'This is the aircraft I would have liked to have designed'
Ernst Heinkel, German aircraft designer

'I wish someone had brought out a wooden aircraft for me'
Hermann Goering, September 1942

'This is the fastest bomber in the world; It must be useful'
Geoffrey de Havilland

THE DE HAVILLAND
MOSQUITO
HISTORY OF A LEGEND

Mike Lepine

SONA BOOKS

sona BOOKS

© Danann Media Publishing Limited 2023

First Published Danann Publishing Ltd 2023

WARNING: For private domestic use only, any unauthorised Copying, hiring, lending or public performance of this book is illegal.

CAT NO: SON0561

Photography courtesy of

Getty images:

Galerie Bilderwelt Popperfoto Royal Air Force Museum
Hulton Archive / Hulton Deutsch Imperial War Museums Corbis Historical
The National Archives Bettmann
Chris McLoughlin Fox Photos / Stringer

All other images, Wiki Commons

Cover design Darren Grice at Ctrl-d

Book layout & design Alex Young at Cre81ve

Cameron Thurlow Copy Editor

All rights reserved. No Part of this title may be reproduced or transmitted in any material form (including photocopying or storing it in any medium by electronic means and whether or not transiently or incidentally to some other use of this publication) without the written permission of the copyright owner, except in accordance with the provisions of the Copyright, Designs and Patents Act 1988. Applications for the copyright owner's written permission should be addressed to the publisher.

Made in EU.
ISBN: 978-1-915343-23-9

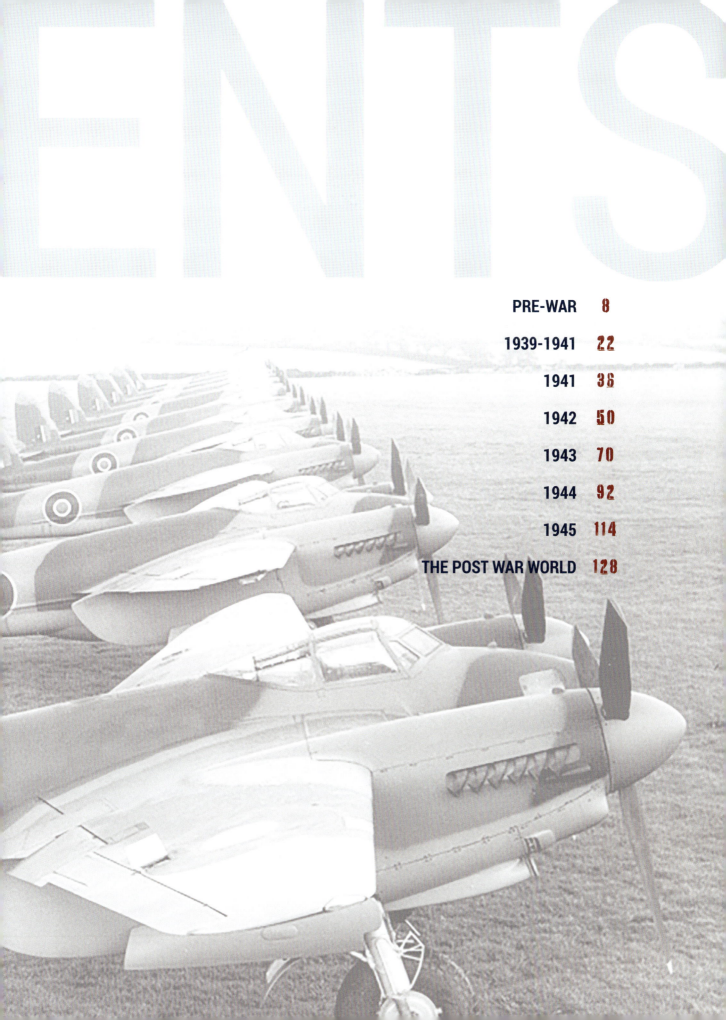

PRE-WAR	8
1939-1941	22
1941	36
1942	50
1943	70
1944	92
1945	114
THE POST WAR WORLD	128

PRE-

'We believe that we could produce a twin-engine bomber which would have a performance so outstanding that little defensive equipment would be needed'

Geoffrey de Havilland, September 1939

The de Havilland Mosquito was first conceived as a bomber, but it soon proved to be very much more. It became, beyond argument, the most versatile aircraft of the Second World War. Some would go as far as to claim it was the finest aircraft of the war. But it very nearly died at the concept stage, like so many of the British aviation industry's greatest contributions to the war effort…

MANUFACTURER VERSUS MINISTRY

Geoffrey de Havilland did not hold a high opinion of the Men from the Ministries — and they weren't much fussed about him. When he could, he and his company avoided them. While designing the Mosquito, they would go as far as to actively hide from them. The Air Ministry meddled. That appeared to be their sole raison d'etre. They bickered, they backstabbed, they gossiped, they blackballed, they prevaricated and constantly changed their minds about what they wanted. Their aircraft specifications led to botched projects and dog's breakfasts. Geoffrey de Havilland was not partial to them at all.

Geoffrey de Havilland was much more straightforward an individual, someone who grew up during the earliest years of powered flight and who saw the aeroplane as simply the most thrilling and challenging thing of his young life. Born in 1882, the son of a clergyman, de Havilland had been expected to follow his father into the Church, but his obvious mechanical skills quickly led him in another direction entirely. He started out designing motor cars and motor cycles — the other great boys' toys of his time - but his first love remained flight. De Havilland designed his first aeroplane in 1907, with £1,000 scrounged from his grandfather. The project took him two years. The No.1 Biplane as it was called proved to be a proficient taxi-er, but when it took off for the first time it stalled and broke up almost immediately.

ABOVE: De Havilland Mosquito in flight

LEFT: Painting of Geoffrey de Havilland, 1940

'It was a mixture of impatience and sheer will power that finally got the first de Havilland machine off on its first flight - and it was crass ignorance that caused it to come back again, violently and disastrously!' — Geoffrey de Havilland.

Undeterred — and against his mother's expressed wishes - de Havilland went back to his grandfather for more money and set about building his second aeroplane using the engine salvaged from the wreck of his first. This proved a lot more successful — in that in 1910 it took him up several inches above the ground for a short distance. Several flights later, he was confident enough to take his eight month old son Geoffrey Junior up for a flight.

For a man who would spend much of the interwar years dodging the 'Men from the Ministries', it is ironic that he sold his very first successful design to the War Office for £400. Now his career took him on a distinctly military trajectory when he found employment at His Majesty's Balloon Factory at Farnborough. Here he was somewhat cold-shouldered for not playing the game and designing balloons but creating aeroplanes instead — but he ultimately enjoyed the last laugh when the establishment officially became the Royal Aircraft Factory. He continued pioneering aeroplane designs and his next major work, the F.E.2, broke the British altitude record of 10,000 feet in 1912 with this brother Hereward at what passed for the controls.

In May 1914, de Havilland was taken on by Airco in Hendon as a test pilot and aircraft designer for the sum of £600 per year plus royalties. He also became a Lieutenant with the Royal Flying Corps Reserve. Throughout the First World War, he designed a line of early warplanes including the DH 4 light bomber which, co-incidentally, was renowned for its speed which could rival a fighter. Over 4,000 were built and de Havilland received a royalty for every one.

The end of the Great War saw an almost immediate collapse in interest in aviation from the government and ministries. They wanted to enjoy their 'Peace Dividend' and any way, everyone knew that they had just fought *'the war to end all wars'*. By 1920, the RAF had shrunk from a wartime figure of 300,000 men to just 3,280 officers and 25,000 in the ranks, with squadrons reduced from 185 to a mere 29. The Ministry of Munitions set up a Disposal Board to get rid of literally tens of thousands of aeroplanes now surplus to requirements. Spare parts and landing fields were sold at knock down prices too, both to raise cash and to make a political point. The Royal Air Force was only saved from oblivion by promising to offer 'war on the cheap' across the Empire, while aircraft manufacturer after aircraft manufacturer went bust or else turned to producing beer barrels, toilet seats or confectionary just to survive.

De Havilland recognised that there was no immediate future in military aircraft and instead looked to civilian aviation. In 1920 he started the de Havilland Aircraft Company in Edgware, Middlesex and, through the decade, his Moth series of training aircraft (de Havilland was a keen entomologist) - proved a phenomenal success. They set new records time and again. The Tiger Moth became the trainer of choice while the Gipsy Moth was adopted by Amy Johnson for her epic solo flight from England to Australia. At the start of the 1930s, when the company moved to Hatfield, de Havilland became intrigued by the new concept of 'airliners' and created the Dragon series of airliners, the earliest of which could carry up to six passengers and formed the backbone of a fledgling London to Paris air service for the rich and important in the early 1930s.

De Havilland's next major step was to design and build the DH 89 Comet, a two seater twin-engined aircraft intended to take part in the 1934 England-Australia MacRobertson Air Race from Britain to Australia. Of wooden construction and built for speed, it was perhaps the earliest incarnation of what would become the Mosquito. It broke rules, it broke records. Three took part in the Race - including one flown by Amy Johnson - and one of them won. The aircraft caused a stir internationally while the Air Ministry purchased one for evaluation. Sadly, they crashed it, lost all interest and sold what remained for scrap.

ABOVE: De Havilland 4 Biplane above the clouds

LEFT: F.E.2a with original undercarriage

ABOVE: A painting of G-ACSS Grosvenor House

BELOW: De Havilland DH.88 Comet 3-view drawing

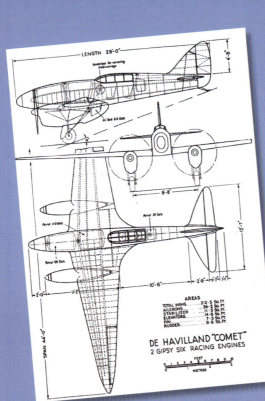

MAIN IMAGE: G-ACSS Grosvenor House at a display by the Shuttleworth Collection

ABOVE: Preserved at the Shuttleworth Collection, one of the original race-tuned Gipsy Six R engines fitted to the winning DH.88 Comet Grosvenor House

RIGHT: Grosvenor House in Martin Place, Sydney, Australia, 12 November 1934

ABOVE: De Havilland D.H.91 Albatross

Continuing his success in civil aviation, de Havilland next conceived the de Havilland DH 91 Albatross, as a transatlantic mail carrier and 22 seat airliner. Designed in 1936, it made its first flight in 1937. Like the Mosquito, its fuselage was of a ply-balsa-plywood sandwich construction and there is little doubt that it contributed significantly to the design of the Mosquito.

While de Havilland enjoyed great success in civil aviation, it seemed like whenever he became involved with the Air Ministry, he came unstuck. The DH 53 Humming Bird trainer, designed to government specification, resulted in just 8 sales to the RAF in the 1920s. The Ministry had also almost completely screwed up his DH 66 Hercules airliner project, trying to get him to design a bomber version and then changing their specification so many times that he gave up. De Havilland's last disastrous experience with the Air Ministry pre-war was to try to meet its Specification T.6/36 specification for a new trainer. The Ministry's spec was technically incompetent, and de Havilland made the mistake of trying to give the Ministry what it was actually asking for. The result was the DH 93 Don, an aircraft that when first flown in 1937, proved as underpowered as it was ill-conceived and undesirable.

A MAN FOR HIS TIME

It was his experience with the Albatross that led Geoffrey de Havilland to start thinking he could build a bomber along much the same lines. Despite his dislike of getting tangled up with the Air Ministry, it was obvious to all that war with Germany was coming and that he had a duty to contribute to the future war effort.

In August 1936, the Air Ministry issued Specification P.13/36 and de Havilland took notice. P.13/36 called for a twin-engined, medium bomber which could carry 3000lb of bombs at 275 mph. It would need an operational ceiling of 15,000 feet. Rival firms started thinking of heavy bombers. De Havilland thought differently. He believed that, given knowledge gained in the building of the Albatross, he could create an aircraft which could exceed the government's specification and be ready in relatively short order because of the advantages of a wooden construction. It was the beginning of the DH 98 project.

At first de Havilland considered straightforwardly adapting the Albatross for use as a bomber. It would have a crew of three and bristled with guns. Early predictions suggested it might carry as much as 6000lb of bombs as far as Berlin at 11,000 feet and at a top speed of 300 mph. It then further occurred to de Havilland that if he cut the size of crew down to two and ditched all the guns, he might well be able to build an aircraft so fast it could race its way out of trouble and therefore not need to be armed at all. Indeed. De Havilland calculated that the guns and gunners added a ton of weight to the design. Without them, this bomber could even outrace the new Spitfire.

This went totally against conventional RAF and Air Ministry thinking. 'The Bomber will always get through' was the maxim of the day and this was seen as only possible because of the sheer power of its guns. America thought the same way. More radical thinking was being practiced in Germany with the idea of the 'evader' or *schnellbomber*. Although carrying defensive weaponry, the Dornier Do.17 had proven itself during the Spanish Civil War usually by outrunning whatever fighters the Republicans could throw at it. The Japanese too at the time were developing an interest in the *schnellbomber* philosophy for their ongoing war against China. The Air Ministry had yet to catch up.

BELOW: De Havilland DH.66 detail drawing from NACA Aircraft Circular No.10

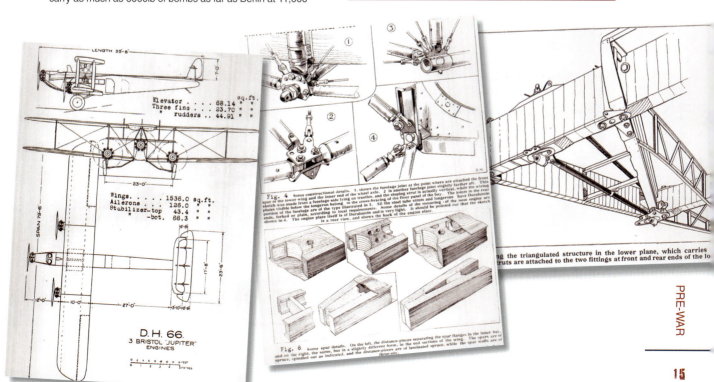

THE PITCH

In October 1938, Sir Geoffrey de Havilland together with Charles Walker, de Havilland's engineering director, were driven the relatively short distance from their Hatfield factory works to the Air Ministry in Whitehall to pitch their new concept.

The pitch was ambitious. De Havilland proposed that his company built a new day bomber which could outrace any fighter. It would be capable of striking at Berlin and would therefore strike fear into the heart of the Third Reich. 1,000 such planes — should the Air Ministry agree — would pose such a threat to Hitler that he might even abandon his plans for war entirely. What's more, the proposed bomber would be made of wood, thus saving precious war materials as well as making it lightweight and devastatingly fast.

The Men from the Ministry were not impressed. The Bristol Blenheim bomber had been sold to them as faster than any fighter, but that was back in the days when it was in competition with the likes of the Gladiator and the Hart. Technology had moved swiftly on and now there were grave doubts about the Blenheim's ability to outrace anything. What's more, no-one was building warplanes from wood any more. It was a well-known fact in intelligence circles that the Germans had already experimented with laminated wood designs and had given it up as a bad job. Administering what they saw as the coup de gras, they told de Havilland that war was most definitely coming soon and it was now too late to pitch anything. It would all be over by the time de Havilland's proposed aircraft made it even to a prototype. The Ministry Men knew that de Havilland had been avoiding government entanglements - and grave doubts were expressed that the company could even cope with the government's complex paperwork during the design process, let alone build anything useful in time. As a good will gesture, it was suggested that de Havilland might instead wish to supply wings for another manufacturer's approved aircraft design instead.

De Havilland and Walker returned to their car somewhat crestfallen. The project seemed over before it had even begun. On the drive back to Hatfield, de Havilland seemed to be wrestling with his thoughts. Finally, he turned to his companion and said, *'we'll do it anyway.'*

LEFT: Sir Geoffrey de Havilland

'(The Mosquito is) a frail wood machine totally unsuitable for Service conditions'

British Air Ministry

FREEMAN'S FOLLY

It was wrong to say that de Havilland had no friends at the Air Ministry. There was one. Air Chief Marshal Sir Wilfrid Freeman was then serving as the Air Member of the Air Council for Development and Production. A tough and bloody-minded Scot, Freeman also possessed a deeply independent and eccentric streak which saw him, among other things, redesign his own RAF uniform to be more to his liking. As a young man, he had served with the Royal Flying Corps during World War One, during which time he became particularly impressed with de Havilland's DH 4 bomber. The aircraft had easily kept pace with any enemy fighter while in service. Freeman thought that if de Havilland could deliver such an aircraft once, he might well be capable of doing it again. He was on board.

Freeman ignored the laughter behind his back at the Ministry and the suggestions that the nameless new aircraft be christened *'Freeman's Folly'*. In private, he told de Havilland to proceed with the project and he'd get them their official order just as soon as he could.

ABOVE: Air Chief Marshal Sir Wilfrid Freeman

BELOW: Airco DH.4

BELOW: The Air Ministry - Council in session in the Council Chamber at Adastral House, London

ABOVE: De Havilland aircraft factory, Rongotai, Wellington, 1939

1939

'In life you must never give up'

Geoffrey de Havilland

In mid-September 1939, de Havilland wrote to Freeman telling him what he could expect of the DH 98. It would offer a range of 1500 miles at a top speed of 405 mph at 18,500 feet and carry either two 500lb or four 250 lb bombs. Now, it just had to be designed.

SALISBURY HALL

Geoffrey de Havilland decided that he would personally finance the project. It was a risk, but he was far from the only British aircraft manufacturer to keep calm and carry on when faced with Air Ministry disinterest. The money would not be a problem — but the Men from the Ministry might be. When they inevitably found out about what he was doing, he knew he could expect all manner of unannounced and unscheduled visits by Ministry Men to Hatfield. They would snoop around, interfere, make unhelpful suggestions, depress his designers and generally cause nothing but trouble. He decided then not to design his new aircraft at Hatfield but at a hidden location.

1941

De Havilland's new aircraft would come to life at Salisbury Hall, a small stately home just five miles from the de Havilland Hatfield works but far enough away. It had its own moat, which was strewn with lilies, and in spring the grounds were blessed with a bed of yellow crocuses. It was charming, very English and seemingly removed from the world.

Built in the 17th Century, Salisbury Hall already possessed a history of subterfuge and intrigue. King Charles II would entertain his mistress Nell Gwyn there in secret, installing her in a nearby cottage to be available to him on demand. According to legend, she remained behind when her lover went on to glory and now haunted the premises. In recent times, it had been home to Sir Nigel Gresley, designer of the record-beating A4 Pacific steam locomotives which brought an inherited air of British engineering excellence to the premises. His most famous design, the Mallard, was named after the ducks he saw swimming in Salisbury Hall's moat.

Winston Churchill had spent time there as a teenager, fishing away the hours in the moat. It was said that one of his catches — a magnificent pike — remained behind at the house. It had been stuffed and framed behind glass, and now held pride of place hung in one of Salisbury Hall's toilets. Legend has it that this pike's strong lines would influence the final shape and design of what was to be the Mosquito.

De Havilland's design team finally moved in on 5 October 1939, under the leadership of Chief Designer R E Bishop

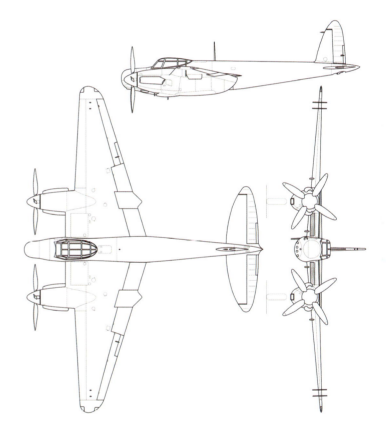

ABOVE: Line drawing of de Havilland Mosquito

LEFT: Salisbury Hall - Former home of Nell Gwyn (allegedly), Jenny Churchill (Winston's mum), Sir Nigel Gresley (designer of the Flying Scotsman and Mallard steam engines), and de Havilland's DH98 Mosquito bomber design office

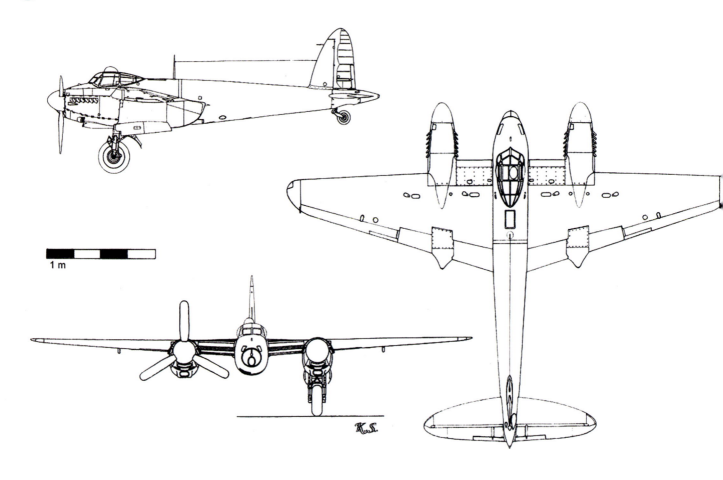

(who had helped to design the world-beating Comet Racer). Up went the drawing boards in the hall's ballroom and the design team settled down to working arduous six and a half day weeks. The kitchen was the province of one Mrs Ledeboer, Bishop's secretary, who doubled as cook and den mother for the design team. She specialised in endless cups of tea for the boys and dinners that were very often fish, which she insisted was 'good for their brains'.

Salisbury Hall remained a closely guarded secret. Few employees at Hatfield knew anything about it and — when one of the Salisbury Hall designers was stricken with appendicitis - a doctor was only allowed in wearing a blindfold and under strict escort. Work progressed swiftly, with Bishop possessing the extraordinary foresight to draw up plans not only for the unarmed bomber version of the aircraft but also a strike version with four 20mm cannon mounted in the nose.

'THE FASTEST BOMBER IN THE WORLD'

In January 1940, with the preliminary design work done, Freeman made good on his word. He met with Geoffrey de Havilland at the Air Ministry to pour over detailed drawings for the Mosquito. *'This is the fastest bomber in the world',* de Havilland announced proudly but defensively. *'It must be useful.'* Freeman agreed. He authorised a prototype to be build and had a specification drawn up the very same

ABOVE: 3-side view of a DH Mosquito PR XVI without drop tanks

day. It was designated BI/40 and would be an unarmed bomber with photo reconnaissance possibilities De Havilland was delighted of course, but also understood that the ministry would now demand snooping rights and the haven of tranquillity that had once been Salisbury Hall was coming to an end. All the old arguments too were bound to be brought up again, including defensive armament and a larger crew.

A small hangar was duly built on the premises of Salisbury Hall and made to look like a barn. Inside was where the new prototype would be built under the auspices of Fred Plumb, Experimental Shop Superintendent. It was accessed by a tricky rope bridge over the moat — and more than one member of staff took an early bath while trying to negotiate it. Later, a second 'barn' would be built on site and Nell Gwyn's cottage unceremoniously turned into a raw materials store.

The Mosquito, as the plane was now being called, was on its way. The prototype was to have a wingspan of 55 feet ten inches and a fusilage constructed of a plywood-balsa-plywood sandwich around a wooden pattern, over which doped fabric would be stretched. The two-man crew would sit side by side in the cockpit, the pilot accommodated on the port side with his navigator to starboard. The plane would be powered by two Rolls Royce Merlin engines.

THE MINISTRY STRIKES BACK

Almost the moment that word got out at the Air Ministry that Freeman had authorised a prototype of his folly, a good deal of peevishness was expressed. It had been assumed that the Ministry had successfully quashed de Havilland's dream aircraft, but their views had been swept aside. A grudging acceptance emerged from Whitehall, followed by an insatiable desire to interfere. Directives for 'modifications' and 'improvements' began to hail down upon Hatfield. The old question of turrets and gunners re-emerged. Tongues wagged. Hobbyhorses were ridden into battle.

Despite the mean-spirited opposition, de Havilland got his first proper contract (69990) on 1 March 1940 for an initial production run of 50 bomber/reconnaissance DH 98s.

ABOVE: De Havilland DH-98 cockpit

'I've got the Mosquito built-ish'

Geoffrey de Havilland, early July 1940

THE DARKEST HOURS

In the Arcadian days of the 'Phony War', there seemed that there was ample time for the Air Ministry to dabble with the Mosquito's design to their heart's content. It was even thought good sport to stick in an oar or a boot. May 1940 brought an abrupt end to that luxury and forced new realities onto planners. The Germans launched a *'Blitzkrieg'* attack on France and the Low Countries and within a month Britain's closest allies had been crushed into submission. The British Expeditionary Force was forced to evacuate at Dunkirk and the invasion of Britain itself now seemed imminent. Time was a luxury that had just run out.

Lord Beaverbrook, appointed by Churchill as Minister of Air Production, insisted that every resource be devoted to the production of Spitfires and Hurricanes for home defence. There would be some allowance to build Wellington, Whitley and Blenheim bombers but there was definitely no spare resources that could be given to developing projects such as the Mosquito, which was not expected to be available for another 18 months. Work at de Havilland on their new prototype ceased almost overnight and de Havilland were instead instructed to mend damaged Hurricanes and even to find ways to fit bomb racks onto their Tiger Moth biplane trainers, such was the shortage of fighting aircraft. Three times Beaverbrook told Freeman to cancel the Mosquito project altogether, but his failure to put his orders in writing gave Freeman the loophole he needed to ignore him.

RIGHT: A de Havilland Mosquito Under Construction

1939-1941

Freeman fought on for the Mosquito project. Such was the threat of invasion that the Air Chief Marshal kept a gangster-style tommy gun in his office, and his fellows at the Ministry joked that he might well turn it on Lord Beaverbrook himself if he didn't relent about the Mosquito. Either by the power of de Havilland's arguments — or the threat of being mown down in a hail of lead like a common mobster — Beaverbrook's mind was quite swiftly changed. Most likely it was the promise from de Havilland in July 1940 that Beaverbrook could have his fifty Mosquitos by mid-1941 - that and the fact that it would put very few demands on the aircraft industry, being made of wood that finally swung it in de Havilland's favour. (In the event de Havilland only managed to deliver 20 of the fifty promised aircraft by the end of 1941). Later that same month — with the Battle of Britain being fought out overhead — and making fighters very desirable, de Havilland was also permitted to go ahead with developing a fighter version.

RULING THE WAVES

One of the earliest roles conceived for the Mosquito fighter was that of providing convoy protection in the stretch of Atlantic west of Ireland as ships were being menaced by Fw 200 Condor long range bombers in the area. In the event, this job first went to Hurricanes launched off catapult-mounted merchant ships and then later to aircraft from escort carriers.

THE BOMBING

The Battle of Britain considerably slowed progress at Hatfield. Bombs fell within a mile of the factory once every five days on average and it's estimated that employees had to spend a full quarter of their working hours stuck in air raid shelters. Although the Germans had no idea about Salisbury Hall at the time, the site was accidentally bombed once when a giant magnetic mine was dropped by parachute and blew off course. It contained enough explosive to devastate Salisbury Hall but by great good fortune its parachute became entangled in the upper branches of a tree and the warhead never came to touch the ground. It was subsequently diffused, hanging by a few threads.

RIGHT: Observer Corps aircraft spotter on the roof of a building in London during the Battle of Britain, with St. Paul's Cathedral in the background

LEFT: RAF recruitment poster

LEFT: Exploded detail view of the WWII British de Havilland Mosquito Light Bomber

THE DE HAVILLAND "MOSQUITO" LIGHT BOMBER

This is the fastest aircraft in operational service in the world, and the Royal Air Force's "lightning" low-level daylight attacks on vital Axis war factories, using "Mosquitoes," are well known. The power is provided by two Rolls-Royce "Merlin 21" liquid-cooled motors, each developing 1,280 h.p., which give a top speed of approximately 400 m.p.h.; this is a substantial margin of speed over most German fighters and, consequently, no armament is carried. Accommodation is made for 2,000 lb. of bombs to be housed internally and carried for great distances, as demonstrated by the raids on Berlin.

The "Mosquito" is also used as a long-range day fighter and night intruder with a very formidable armament of four cannon and four machine-guns concentrated in the nose. Other versions are used for photographic reconnaissance and training. A crew of two is carried in this all-wooden fighter-bomber, which has a span of 54 ft. 2 in. and a length of 40 ft. 9½ in.

1 PILOT
2 SECOND PILOT-NAVIGATOR-BOMB-AIMER
3 RADIO RECEIVER AND TRANSMITTER
4 FUEL TANKS
5 OIL TANKS
6 ROLLS-ROYCE "MERLIN 21" MOTORS
7 DE HAVILLAND CONSTANT-SPEED HYDROMATIC AIRSCREWS
8 ENGINE-COOLING TANK
9 CARBURETTER AIR INTAKE
10 OIL AND COOLING RADIATORS
11 FLAME-TRAP EXHAUSTS
12 FLAP OPERATING-GEAR
13 UNDERCARRIAGE OPERATING-GEAR
14 FLAPS
15 AILERON
16 AILERON TRIM TAB
17 NAVIGATION LIGHT
18 NAVIGATION HEADLAMP
19 BOMB-SIGHT
20 BOMB SELECTOR SWITCHES
21 NAVIGATION TABLE
22 COCKPIT ENTRANCE DOOR
23 BOMB RACK
24 500 LB. BOMBS
25 OXYGEN BOTTLES
26 ACCUMULATORS
27 HIGH-TENSION POWER UNIT
28 PNEUMATIC-GEAR CONTROL-PANEL
29 DINGHY STOWAGE
30 OPERATING GEAR FOR RETRACTABLE TAIL WHEEL
31 FIN AND RUDDER
32 RUDDER MASS BALANCE
33 RUDDER TRIM TAB
34 ELEVATOR
35 ELEVATOR TRIM TAB
36 TAIL NAVIGATION LIGHT
37 PITOT HEAD

Although the threat of invasion had passed by October 1940, German raiders still flew almost daily bombing missions over Britain. On the morning of 3 October 1940, it was Hatfield's turn to be on the receiving end.

Shortly before 11.30am a lone Ju 88 bomber dropped out of low rain clouds close to the Hatfield factory and swept in on its bombing run through a shroud of ground fog at tree-top height. Inexperienced observers on the factory roof initially thought it was a British aircraft coming in to make an unscheduled landing and so vital time was lost raising the alarm. Confusion turned to concern as the aircraft got closer. The Factory Klaxons sounded and staff began to head for the shelters located inside the factory or the dugout trenches outside.

The Ju 88 strafed the factory as it released its payload of four bombs. Some as they landed actually skidded on the grass airfield and slid and bounced straight into the area known as the 94 Shop, exploding inside and flinging debris 300 feet in the air. One bomb collapsed a shelter onto the staff huddled inside while a second caught factory workers fleeing down a staircase and hurled them into the air.

Anti-aircraft gunners on site opened up on the low level raider. It juddered under fire, peeled away with its starboard engine blazing and crashed into a field. All four crewmen survived and were rounded up by local police before being turned over to British Intelligence. The rumour later emerged that the Junkers' pilot had worked as an apprentice with de Havilland at Hatfield before the war and therefore knew precisely where to find it.

Whether the raid was intended to strike at Hatfield or not, it had fearsome consequences. 21 workers were killed and another 70 injured. The 94 shed had been used to store manufactured Mosquito materials to meet the first order. 80 per cent it of it was destroyed — the equivalent of nine months' work.

FIRST FLIGHT

Fortunately for de Havilland the first prototype of the Mosquito had been assembled at the Salisbury Hall site and was not lost in the bombing raid of 3 October.

Now painted bright yellow and designated EO234 (later W4050), on 3 November 1940, the first Mosquito was disassembled and loaded onto a trailer for its road journey to Hatfield. It completed the journey under a tarpaulin to maintain a shroud of secrecy. Once reassembled at Hatfield, it made its first taxi runs on the grass airstrip there on 24 November. A day later, it took to the air. Geoffrey de Havilland was there to watch. At the controls was Sir Geoffrey's eldest son, Geoffrey Jnr, accompanied by navigator John Walker. The test crew took the Mosquito up to 15,000 feet during a flight lasting 45 minutes. The take-off was recorded as *'straightforward and easy'*. Speeds of 220 mph were achieved and the Mosquito behaved almost flawlessly. No major issues were identified. Manufacturing trials would continue for another three months, during which time the Mosquito logged 38 hours of test flights, achieving a new altitude of 22,000 feet and a top speed of 388 mph.

On the 29 December, Lord Beaverbrook was formally introduced to the Mosquito at a special event held at

ABOVE: Mosquito prototype W4050 landing after a test flight on 10 January 1941: Four test flights were flown that day

LEFT: People in London look at a map illustrating how the RAF is striking back at Germany during 1940

Langley. Geoffrey de Havilland Jnr laid on a spectacular show, buzzing the airfield at 400 mph and even performing a number of upward roles with one engine shut down. As a direct result, the very next day de Havilland received a fresh order for 150 Mosquitos. They were warned to expect *'further extensive orders'* and were strongly advised to find further sites to share the task of manufacture and to further build a network of trusted subcontractors. Less than two weeks later, de Havilland was also instructed to build a prototype for reconnaissance purposes. Of its initial production run of 50 aircraft, de Havilland was told to build 19 reconnaissance planes [including the prototype] and 28 fighters. Bomber variants could follow as part of the further order for 150 aircraft. The Ministry were to change their minds constantly during production. Now they wanted Mosquitos; they just didn't know which type.

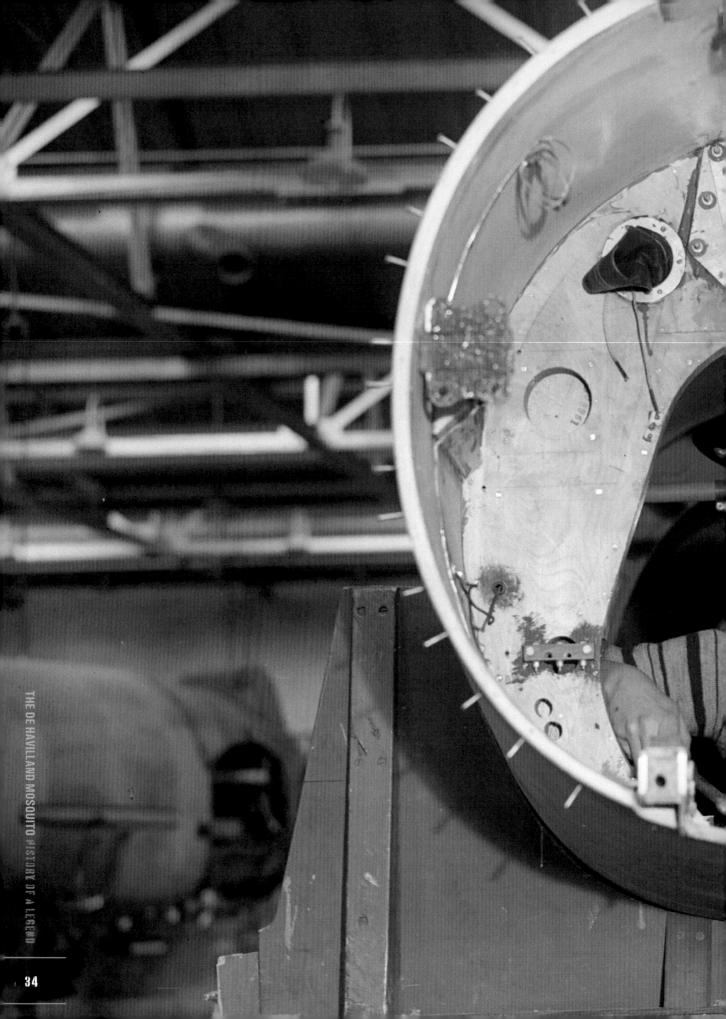

LEFT: A female factory worker solders small parts in the tail section of a Mosquito bomber, the fastest aircraft in operation in the world, 1941

'...pleasant to fly'

Test Pilot report on the Mosquito

On 19 February 1941, the Mosquito prototype was handed over to the RAF to undergo evaluation at the Aeroplane and Armament Experimental Establishment at Boscombe Down. Here, it was initially treated with some bored indifference - and misbehaved for the first time.

RAF test pilots said that it did not handle well and frankly made them nervous. They didn't like the small cramped cockpit (described by one pilot as 'hardly bigger than a large wardrobe'). There was also some buffeting experienced and vibration.. Worst of all, the tail wheel's stubborn refusal to turn resulted in a crack in the fuselage. This meant that the second Mosquito prototype — a photo reconnaissance version — had to be hauled to Boscombe Down and 'cannibalised' to repair the first prototype. De Havilland felt they had just had a lucky escape. They expected that the Ministry would use the accident as an excuse to cancel the Mosquito…

Those testing the machine also expressed their concerns about the lack of armaments and the Air Ministry duly and predictably joined them in support. (Eventually a 4-gun rearward-firing turret was added to a prototype. Test flights resulted in a loss of speed of some 20 mph. As he had throughout the project, de Havilland fiercely resisted the installation of a turret and eventually succeeded in having it removed from future tests).

However, one thing the test crews were enthusiastic about was the top speed recorded during trials — a quite amazing 388 mph at 20,000 feet. Indeed, it came as such a shock that the Ministry requested a double check on the airspeed before they could believe it. For a bomber this was really fast and in tests against a Spitfire, it was found that the Mosquito could out-race it by some 20 mph at 6,000 feet, just as de Havilland had promised. Now the once-critical Ministry Men descended on Boscombe Down in great numbers to get a first look at the plane everyone who was anyone was talking about.

LEFT: General Henry H. Arnold

THE AMERICANS TAKE NOTE

On 20 April 1941, an excited Lord Beaverbrook invited two very special VIPs to see the Mosquito for themselves. They were the US ambassador, John Wynant, and the head of the United States Army Air Corps, General 'Hap' Arnold. During the demonstration the Mosquito achieved 400 mph in level flight. The guests were duly impressed.

ABOVE: American F-8 Mosquito nose; USAAF markings, PRU Blue finish at the National Museum of the United States Air Force

Six days later, a full set of manufacturer's drawings were on their way to Washington. Arnold later recalled:

'The first time I saw the Mosquito (I was) impressed by its performance… (an) airplane that looks fast usually is fast, and the Mosquito was, by the standards of the time, an extremely well-streamlined airplane, and it was highly regarded, highly respected.'

RIGHT: De Havilland Mosquito Mark II

BELOW: De Havilland DH.98 Mosquito MK. IV

LEFT: Airborne Interception Radar: AI Mark VIIIB installed in the nose of a de Havilland Mosquito NF Mark XIII night fighter. The transmitter box is at the top, mounted above the scanner hydraulic motor assembly. The rotating scanner is contained in the perspex nose. Photograph taken at No. 10 Maintenance Unit, Hullavington, Wiltshire. Operating at a frequency of 3 GHz (10 centimeters wavelength) powered by the new magnetron tube invented by John Randall and Harry Boot at Birmingham University, UK in 1940, this was the first microwave air intercept radar, used on British warplanes in World War 2 beginning late 1941

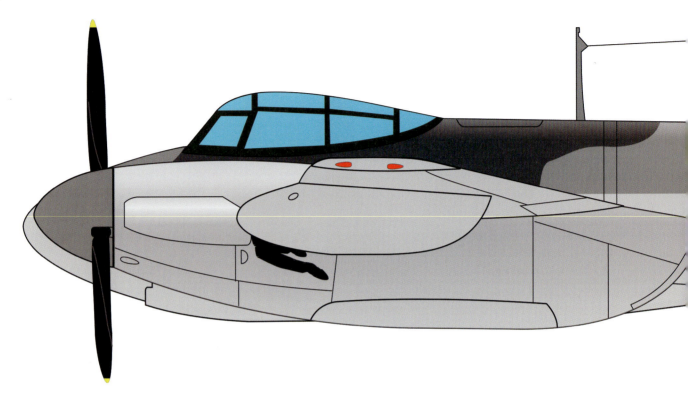

The five American manufacturers asked to evaluate the Mosquito back were less enthusiastic than the General, erroneously suggesting that the Mosquito's wooden frame was a serious drawback instead of a benefit. Some referred to the Mosquito contemptuously as *'the hollowed-out log'*. Self-interest won out against an honest evaluation. Emphasis was given to the P-38 Lockheed Lightning instead and American Mosquito enthusiasts spent much of the rest of the war trying to beg, steal or borrow 'Mozzies' to use with USAAF.

THE SECOND PROTOTYPE

Even as the first prototype was still being put through its trials, Salisbury Hall was hurrying to construct a further prototype, this time a fighter variant designated FII W4052 made to Ministry specification F.21/40. (Although now frequently considered the second prototype, W4052 was actually the third, the second (W4051) having been cannibalised for repairs to W4050 at Boscombe Down).

From the start, the aircraft was conceived primarily as a night fighter to intercept ongoing Luftwaffe bombing raids. Its design incorporated two Rolls Royce Merlin 21 engines and a new bulletproof canopy. It was fitted with four Browning 0.303 machine guns inside a solid nose piece and four 20mm Hispano cannon mounted in the fuselage below the cockpit.

Disassembling and transporting the initial prototype from Salisbury Hall to Hatfield had proved not only time-consuming but also difficult to reassemble at the other end. It was Experimental Shop Superintendent Fred Plumb who suggested converting a field to the rear of the Hall into a makeshift grass airstrip and flying the new prototype out to Hatfield from there. The field proposed was far from ideal. For one thing it sloped quite considerably and for another it ended rather abruptly with a large hawthorn hedge and two sturdy trees. The farmer was far from pleased at the suggesting to demolish the obstacles and in the end relented only enough to allow a small section of the hedge to be ripped out —just enough for the Mosquito to squeeze

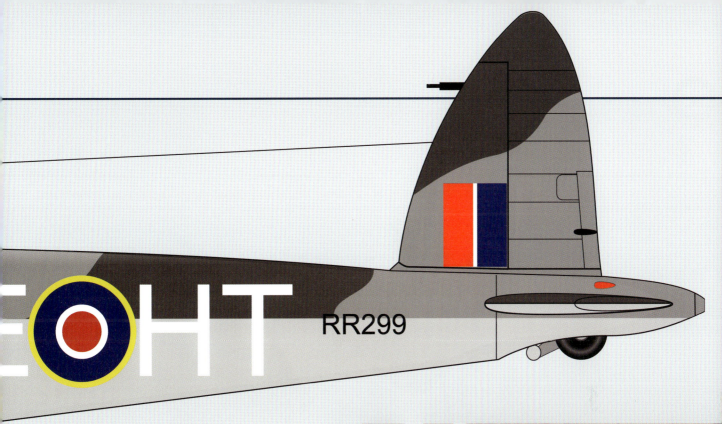

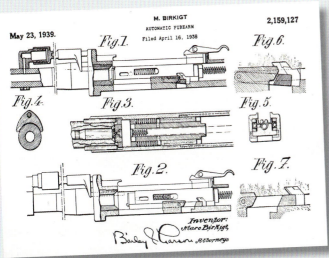

MAIN IMAGE: Illustration of a de Havilland Mosquito

ABOVE: Hispano-Suiza Aircraft Gun, US Patent Drawing 1939

ABOVE RIGHT: A 1,690 hp Rolls Royce Merlin 114 liquid-cooled V12 aero engine with 2-speed, 2-stage supercharger of a de Havilland Mosquito TT35

through. After this had been completed, Geoffrey de Havilland took the aircraft up from the makeshift 450-yard airfield on 15 May with Fred Plumb as his navigator. Plumb had bet him £1 they would never make it. On the way, the cockpit canopy came loose and fell off over Hertfordshire.

Test flights on this prototype at Hatfield began in mid-May 1941 and by 22 June it was on its way to Boscombe Down for evaluation. Tests completed, a month later it was fitted was fitted with longwave airborne intercept Mark IV (AI.IV) radar and became the start of the NFII night fighter mark.

ABOVE: A ground crew sergeant demonstrates the operation of the photo-reconnaissance camera in a de Havilland Mosquito

THE GERMANS GET CURIOUS

Just two days before the second Mosquito prototype was scheduled to head off to Hatfield for trials, a lone German aircraft flew close to the site by night and dropped Oberstturmfuhrer Karel Richter by parachute. The SS officer, dressed in civilian clothes and a natty trilby hat, had been despatched with orders to find out just what was going on at Salisbury Hall. He was walking to the Hall (carrying a portable wireless transmitter) when a lorry driver pulled up and asked for directions. Impatient to be about his task, Richter was abrupt, insulting and rude to the driver — and he did it in an outrageous foreign accent. Quite naturally, the driver went straight to the police and reported him as a spy. Richter was quickly apprehended by the police and then tried and executed that December.

THE THIRD PROTOTYPE

Having been laboriously repaired after being cannibalised to make W4050 airworthy, the Photo Reconnaissance version of the Mosquito — W4051 — finally took off on its maiden flight on 10 June 1941. This new version could carry a wide range of camera equipment and would eventually feature an extra 700 gallon tank in what would otherwise have been the bomb bay. Such was the excitement generated now by the Mosquito that two days into the tests the commanding officer of No 1 Photographic Reconnaissance Unit, RAF, turned up in person at Hatfield to and wangled himself a test flight. On 25 June it went off to Boscombe Down.

FIGHTER-BOMBER

In July 1941, Salisbury Hall commenced design work on yet another version of the Mosquito, this time a fighter-bomber version combining the fighter version's Hispano cannon and Browning machine guns with a capability to carry a 1,000lb bomb. It would be the version everyone wanted.

IN DEMAND

Once the Mosquito had truly proved itself at Boscombe Down, orders flooded from a Ministry which had once been so sceptical and dismissive. In short order, the Havilland's Hatfield factory simply could not keep up with demand for the aircraft and the decision was taken to turn the company's manufacturing facilities at nearby Leavesden near Watford over to the Mosquito. The main Hatfield plant, it was agreed, would specialise in producing the bomber and photoreconnaissance versions while Leavesden produced the airframes for fighter and forthcoming fighter-bomber versions. The nearby Aldenham bus depot was seconded into service as an overspill area for fuselage production. Even with the addition of an extra factory, de Havilland still could not keep up with the orders and more Mosquito manufacturing sites had to be sourced. These included Standard Motors at Coventry and Luton's Percival Aircraft.

ABOVE: Four Browning machine guns

> '*The drive to increase and expand went out like a great crusade, carried into the byways by teams of car-driving contact men who, despite fires, blast and craters, poor tyres and petrol coupons, struggled to build up the output from hundreds of suppliers*'
>
> From an article in the de Havilland Gazette, September 1945.

BELOW: An engineer at work on a de Havilland Mosquito British warplane

THE NATION JOINS IN

There were over 400 sub-contractors sourced to supply pieces of the Mosquito to the main construction facilities, from coach builders and manufacturers of fine wooden furnishings (the Mosquito had been sneered at in the past as 'Flying Furniture') to clutches of old ladies beavering away in the garden shed. Small villages pooled their sources to manufacture a specialist component, and it was not unheard of for a family to convert a room in their home to turn out a piece, if approved by the Ministry of Aircraft Production. One woman, who had given over her drawing room to constructing a minor part, recalled that her improvised 'production line' included everyone from duchesses to charladies. Even Decca Records joined in.

CANADIAN MOSQUITOS

In July 1941, de Havilland Mosquito began preparations to have Mosquitos built at their subsidiary Downsview factory close to Toronto in Canada. Initial expectations were for 40 aircraft a month, rising to 50 a month by 1943. Engines for the Canadian Mosquitos would initially be supplied from Britain but after 270 Mosquitos had been completed, their engines were switched over to be fitted with Rolls-Royce Merlin specification by American engineering specialists Packard.

Assemblies and technical drawings followed by sea, but many were lost on the way because of U-Boats which undoubtedly slowed the preparations down. To solve this problem it was decided that Downsview would build its own jigs and moulds — but this would take precious time. Meanwhile, the company had an initial order from the Ministry of Aircraft production for 400 aircraft which they could not fulfil.

The factory received a further order for 1,100 Mosquitos in Spring 1942 and full scale production finally began in September that year. At first Downsview specialised in the bomber variant but then added the fighter-bomber to its

production lines in 1943. The dual control trainer variant would follow in good time.

It was not until August 1943 that the first five Canadian Mosquitos were flown across the Atlantic via Greenland and Iceland to enter into RAF service. To make the transatlantic flight, they were fitted with 200 gallon fuel tanks stowed in the bomb bay. This proved to be a hazardous operation and resulted in a significant loss of aircraft during ferrying. Pilots were consequently paid $1000 'danger money' per transatlantic flight. Some losses

were blamed on the phenomenon of 'auto explosion'. A number of the aircraft simply vanished and what brought them down has never been known..

1034 Mosquitos would eventually be built at Downsview. All of them bore the XX on their mark to distinguish them as Canadian-built. By 1945, production was so successful that spare fuselages exceeded demand and they remained stacked up in the corner of a warehouse. It is reputed that a local prostitute used one of the fuselages to discreetly ply her trade in, and soon those in the know would whisper '*second fuselage from the end!*' to those new to her charms.

ABOVE: Assembly workers attached plywood sheets to one half of the fuselage section shell of a de Havilland DH98 Mosquito twin-engined multirole fighter-bomber aircraft during construction of the aircraft for service with the Royal Air Force at the Walter Lawrence & Sons, Joinery Works in Sawbridge, Hertfordshire

With the success of the Canadian operation, plans began to be drawn up for an Australian manufacturing operation, as Japan had just entered the war, but this was to amount to little until 1943.

EARLY OPERATIONS

Mosquitos had started to be delivered to 1PRU In July of 1941. The aircraft, designated PR I, were based on the bomber airframe and carried cameras and extra-fuel tanks to extend their range. They were painted sky blue to help avoid detection at altitude. The Mosquito was still particularly hard to get hold of at this stage however, and RAF Coastal Command's No.1 Photographic Reconnaissance Unit only had five in total at the time they flew their first combat sortie. The next two to be received would have the bonus of extra range, their fuel tanks having a capacity of 700 gallons compared with the first models, which could only carry a maximum of 500 gallons.

Unfortunately, the first Mosquito operation of the Second World War was sabotaged — by a bee. The unarmed aircraft, W4055, which belonged to 1PRU was despatched from Benson in Oxfordshire on a mission over Brest and

the Spanish border on 17 September 1941. The pilot was Squadron Leader Rupert Clarke —the Eton-educated step-son of Air Chief Marshall Sir Edgar Ludlow-Hewitt. The navigator was Sergeant Sowerbutts — a hairdresser from Margate. While on their way to their target, they began to experience technical difficulties which caused Clarke to abandon the mission. Later it was discovered that a bee had climbed into the plane's pitot tube, causing its airspeed indicator to go haywire at 24,000 feet. The cameras also failed to operate.

The first successful sortie was actually flown on 20 September 1941 over Heligoland by Flight Lieutenant Alastair Taylor. He flew Mosquito W4055 — the same aircraft that had been used on the aborted first sortie. Three Bf 109 fighters were sent up to intercept the Mosquito but their pilots were astonished to find they couldn't catch it. Just ten weeks after that, the same pilot had the misfortune to also fly the first Mosquito lost in combat, after being shot down by enemy anti-aircraft fire over Trondheim, Norway. His navigator, Sergeant Horsfall, was also killed.

LEFT: A Mosquito being tested at the de Havilland factory

1942

'Pressure is a Messerschmitt up your arse, playing cricket is not'

Keith Miller - Legendary Australian cricketer and ex-Mosquito pilot,
on being asked how he remained so calm on the cricket pitch

INCREASED ORDERS

At the end of January 1942, the Air Ministry further increased their order. Now it was requested that 928 Mosquitos be supplied from Hatfield and a further 450 from Leavesden. 400 more were to be sourced from Canada. The variants were not specified, but the order served as an advanced warning. Predictably, the Ministry of Aircraft Supply kept changing their minds about what they wanted throughout the entire year, as well as persistently interfering in the production process.

THE MOSQUITO TRAINER

To help 'convert' aircrew from their old aircraft to the new Mosquito, a number of T III dual control trainers were built. The first flew on 30 January 1942. These were unarmed and powered by Merlin 21 or 23/25 engines. A total of 362 were built for service with the RAF and the Fleet Air Arm. Most of them originated at the Leavesden factory but a limited number were also built at Hatfield.

Variants were built in Canada as well as in Australia. Canada produced six T 22 trainers with Packard-Merlin 33 engines and then a further 19 T 27 trainers with Packard-Merlin 225 engines. Australia produced its own version, the T 43, with 22 being constructed in all.

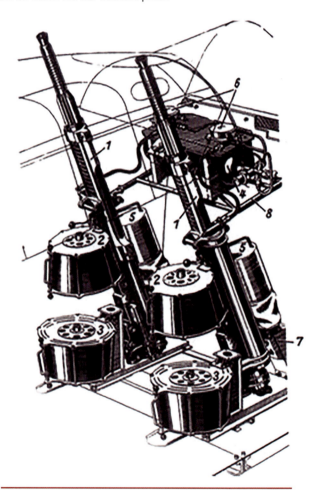

ABOVE: Interior view of Messerschmitt Bf 110G-4 Schräge Musik installation: 1. MG FF/M 2. Main drums 3. Reserve drums 4. Pressurized container with pressure-reducing gear and stop valve 5. Spent cases container 6. FPD and FF (Radio installation) 7. Weapon mount 8. Weapon recoil dampener

RECONNAISSANCE OPS – EARLY 1942

By the spring of 1942, Coastal Command Mosquitos from No1. Photographic Reconnaissance Unit — mostly flying from Wick and Leuchars in Scotland (but also from St. Eval down in Cornwall) were confidently operating up to ten sorties every day of the week ranging all over Scandinavia and continental Europe. Some even flew as far as Poland and Czechoslovakia.

The missions were mostly flown to provide up to date target information for Bomber Command as well as to keep track of predacious German warships. It was Mosquito W4051 — the actual reconnaissance prototype — that flew on the op that located the German battlecruiser *Gneisenau* in dry dock in Kiel on 22 February 1942. Diversionary flights were also flown so as not to give the Germans advanced notice of forthcoming targets.

When the weather was favourable, the optimum ceiling on photo reconnaissance ops in the Mosquito was quickly established at 22,000 feet, but in the event of bad weather Mosquitos were known to descend to as low as 400 feet to complete their mission.

Mosquitos were first used to record the aftermath of a Bomber Command raid on 4 March 1942. The previous night, the Renault factory in Paris had been bombed. Hampered by heavy rain, the Mosquito was forced to drop right down to 400ft over the River Seine to obtain photographs.

Ten Mosquito PR Is were built in total,. The last of these were special. 'Tropicalized' long range versions which

ABOVE: A Rolls-Royce Merlin engine

ABOVE: No. 23 Squadron flew Mosquito NF II Specials on night intruder operations from Malta

were despatched to Malta and Egypt in January of 1942. The Maltese Mosquito was lost while flying an operation over Italy. It was intercepted by a Bf 109 and badly shot up. None the less, the crew managed to nurse their stricken aircraft back to base and both survived the crash-landing.

In excess of 30 Mosquito B IV bombers were also converted into the PR IV photo-reconnaissance versions and start flying in that role from April 1942. A further number of Mosquito night fighters were also converted for use by the PRU, such was the demand.

THE FIRST BOMBING MISSIONS

The Mosquito bomber was first delivered to 2 Light Bomber Group, where it was to replace the Blenheim. The initial aircraft was delivered on 15 November 1941 by Geoffrey de Havilland Jnr. personally. To give the crews below a taste of what they were about to fly, he put on a daredevil show of aerobatics and low level, high speed runs across the aerodrome before coming into land. (Sadly, this historic aircraft developed faults the very next day and had to be sent back to the factory). The second Mosquito was delivered two days after, and three more followed in close order just before 2 Light Bomber Group moved to its new home at Horsham St. Faith, close to Norwich in Norfolk.

There was next to no training available for bomber pilots to convert from the Blenheim to the Mosquito and most received around an hour of flying with an instructor before being allowed to go solo. Some pilots were merely shown around the aircraft before being able to take it up unaccompanied. Nevertheless, the airmen took to the Mosquito almost immediately and raced around the skies of East Anglia on practice flights just above the treetops, terrifying the locals and livestock.

There were meant to be two Mosquito bomber squadrons fully operational by the summer of 1942 — 105 and 139 Squadrons. However such was the shortage of available planes that 139 Squadron were forced to beg, steal or borrow any available aircraft from 105 Squadron to conduct many of its operations. Not that 105 Squadron itself was spoiled for planes; By mid-May 1942, just seven Mosquitos had been delivered to the squadron — six B 1s (converted from the PR or photo reconnaissance version) and a solitary B IV Series II. They however become the pioneers of radical Mosquito low level bombing tactics for other squadrons to follow. In less than a year, 105 Squadron would lose 35 aircraft in low level daylight raids, learning painful but essential lessons.

It was Squadron Leader Alan Robertson Oakeshott who led the very first Mosquito bombing raid of the war on 31 May. The night before, 1,000 British bombers had struck at Cologne. Now four unarmed Mosquitos from 105 Squadron were ordered to head to the city even as the heavy bombers came home. Their mission was to keep the pressure up on Cologne by bombing it in broad daylight from high altitude. In essence, it was a 'nuisance raid' — the first of many to be conducted by Mosquitos over the course of the war. The city was almost obscured in boiling black cloud rising up to 14,000 feet as the mosquitos arrived individually to drop their payloads of one 500lb bomb and two 250 lb bombs. Dead reckoning had to be used as the target was so obscured. One Mosquito failed to return to base, the victim of flak.

139 Squadron joined the action on 25 June by launching a low level strafing raid on the airfield at Stade near Wilhelmshaven. Now promoted to Wing Commander and placed in charge of 139 Squadron, Alan Oakeshott led a five Mosquito raid against the U-boat yards at Flensberg on 2 July. It was an ambitious mission — and it failed. Two of the five Mosquitos were lost. The unarmed bombers were intercepted by both Focke Wulf Fw190 and Bf 109 fighters, and the Mosquito crews' inexperience was to prove lethal. Oakeshott's own Mosquito was attacked by an Fw 190 and brought down over the North Sea. Both he and his navigator were lost. Horsham St. Faith's base commander, Group Captain J C MacDonald, was also shot down on the raid, although he and his navigator both survived to become prisoners of war.

Flensberg was a shock to the novice Mosquito crews and doubts about the aircraft began to emerge, particularly about sending it out unarmed. Tests began on fitting a rear-mounted gun. None of the methods proposed were satisfactory. There was also concern about the Luftwaffe's Fw 190 fighters, which Mosquito crews had taken to calling '*snappers*'. They were fast — fast enough to directly challenge the Mosquito. Tests on a captured Fw 190 showed that the Mosquito held a speed advantage of just 5 mph. Behind the scenes, experiments began to somehow restore the Mosquito's speed advantage. These included a high polish finish (which added 5 mph to the plane's speed) and new exhausts (10-13 mph). No-one was sure either of the wisdom of low level daylight attacks — at altitudes of just 100 feet or so. In short, no-one yet knew the best way to use the Mosquito against the enemy.

Nevertheless, nine days later six Mosquitos from Horsham St. Faith' returned to Flensburg to exact revenge. The Mosquitos came in at ultra-low level, in two waves of three aircraft. The first wave successfully hit the target with high explosives and incendiaries, but the second wave fell apart. One aircraft became separated and returned to base. A second flew so low that it sheared off a chimney pot which ricocheted off the port engine, bounced and ripped a massive hole in the fuselage before quite literally ending up on the navigator's lap. The unnerved crew were forced to abort. A third Mosquito was shot down. The second raid hardly restored confidence in the Mosquito.

ABOVE: Lt. Col. Elliott Roosevelt

There was only one way to do that. They would fly an even more difficult raid. On 19 September 1942 six Mosquitos from Horsham St Faith flew across almost the whole of Germany to deliver the first-ever daylight raid on Berlin. This time, high altitude was chosen for the bombing run but as the city was mostly covered by cloud, it was never determined what damage to the capital the Mosquitos had caused, if any. One aircraft failed to return.

THE MOSQUITO ABROAD

While the efficacy of the Mosquito bomber remained mired in doubt, the PR version was now receiving almost universal accolades. Everyone with photo reconnaissance responsibilities wanted them now — and in quantity. Mosquitos for example were shipped out to Gibraltar and from there conducted important PR missions over North Africa. In November 1942, Mosquitos from Gibraltar flew vital reconnaissance missions for Operation Torch (the invasion of French North Africa) and successfully evaded attacks by French fighters working for the Germans.

AMERICAN INTEREST

One of the three Mosquito PR's based in Gibraltar was gifted to Colonel Elliott Roosevelt. He was head of an American photo reconnaissance unit in North Africa — and also the son of President Roosevelt. Almost immediately, he recognised that the Mosquito was a great improvement over the P 38 Lightning that he was used to flying and stuck his nose up at the US aviation industry by telling the world that he would happily swap a squadron of P 38s for a Squadron of the British Mosquitos. A new interest grew in Washington, with General Arnold once more resuming his mission to get the Americans to buy British. Unfortunately there were still too few Mosquitos to even meet the RAF's demands and Arnold was unable to get the Air Ministry to spare any even when he offered to swap P 51 Mustangs for the Mozzies. Wilfred Freeman, the Mosquito's original champion, was secretly delighted. In private, he said that the Americans didn't have any planes worth swapping Mosquitos for anyway.

THE FIRST MOSQUITO FIGHTERS

In January 1941, de Havilland had been told to include 28 fighter versions of the Mosquito in its existing order. The W4053 prototype for the fighter variant actually included a rear firing turret. On its first flight, bits of the turret fell off.

As a day fighter, the Mosquito was initially ill at ease. It packed the powerful punch of four Hispano cannon and four .303 Browning machine guns which made it more than capable of bringing down anything, but it lacked the sheer agility and rate of climb necessary to take on something single-engined like the Fw 190 in a straightforward daytime dogfight. Its very speed threatened to work against it. When closing on a much slower target, the Mosquito tended to overshoot the enemy, prematurely ending the interception. Air brakes were considered, but in the end

ABOVE: Warrant Officer D Gosling (left) and Squadron Leader G H Hayhurst of No. 604 Squadron RAF, stand in front of their de Havilland Mosquito NF Mark XII in the snow at B51/Lille-Vendeville, France, before taking off on a night-fighter sortie

it was found that manipulating the wing flaps to slow the plane on its intercept worked best.

The first Mosquitos joined Fighter Command in January 1942.

NIGHT FIGHTER

The Mosquito NF superseded the Bristol Blenheim as the main defender of Britain's night skies in 1942. The first was delivered to 157 Squadron based at RAF Castle Camps in Cambridgeshire in January 1942. By mid-April 1942, squadron strength had increased to twenty aircraft and 157 were ready to go operational. All aircraft were painted matte black for night ops — an essential feature which, nonetheless, shaved as much as 26 mph off their top speed. They were joined by 151 Night Fighter Squadron based in Northants, that squadron receiving its first Mosquito NF on 6 April.

In combat, Mosquito NF's were vectored onto targets by CGI ground radar, before using their on-board sets to close in. The NF II was fitted with AI Mk IV metric wavelength airborne radar in the nose.

Despite flying sorties from late April 1942, it took until the night of 24-25 June before the Mosquito NF achieved its first confirmed kill. Wing Commander Irving Stanley Smith, CO of 151 Squadron, succeeded in bringing down two Dornier 217 bombers in a single night. Across spring and summer 1942, more Mosquito night fighter squadrons joined the fight, and achieved an increasingly impressive number of kills. The Luftwaffe's response was to fly over Fw 190 A-4 and A-5s, converted to carry a single bomb. They attacked targets throughout the south east of England, forcing Fighter Command to redeploy 157 and 85 Squadrons to the area. Now flying NF XIIs, they proved more than adequate in intercepting the Nazi raiders, bringing down four in just one night on 16-17 May.

By the time the Mosquito came in as a night fighter, Luftwaffe night raids over Britain were diminishing and more and more emphasis began to be placed on flying night intruder raids over Occupied Europe instead of defending the home skies. Some special versions were also built, omitting the radar in favour of extra fuel tanks for long range attack duties and aircraft of this type, designated NF II (Special), were used with distinction by 23 Squadron to conduct raids over occupied Europe and later the Mediterranean..

During the war Mosquito NF variants were responsible for the destruction of over 600 German aircraft. A total of 466 would be built in all.

WAR AT HIGH ALTITUDE

In the summer of 1942, the Luftwaffe quite suddenly presented a new daytime threat, sending over the Ju 86P, a militarised version of a pre-war pressurised airliner design capable of high altitude flight at 39,000ft. A Spitfire sent to intercept one such raid simply could not reach the altitude. The bomber was not capable of carrying much of a payload but it did fly over sensitive areas — including de Havilland's own Hatfield factory.

The decision was swiftly taken to develop a Mosquito fighter variant capable of reaching — and neutralising — the new threat. To help it reach the height needed, the wingspan was increased, fuel tanks were reduced and some defensive armour plating done away with. Merlin 61 engines were selected and the cockpit pressurised. The initial redesign took de Havilland just seven days. This variant, designated the MP 469, proved capable of reaching an astounding altitude of 43,500 feet and was delivered for service at RAF Northolt. Joining MP 469 were four B IVs which were converted into NF XVs.

Trials stretched into mid-1943, by which time the threat of the Ju 86P had largely passed, but work continued on the high altitude Mosquito as it was foreseen that high flying Luftwaffe night fighters might poses a threat in the near future.

BELOW: The prototype Mosquito NF Mark XV, MP469

INTRUDERS

As 1942 progressed, the Luftwaffe were forced to devote more and more of their aircraft to the Eastern Front. Raids on Britain became significantly rarer. With so little 'trade' to be had In the night skies at home, more and more Mosquito night fighters were used for 'Intruder' missions from May 1942 onwards, hunting enemy aircraft in the skies over Europe. With their high speed, formidable firepower and extended range capability, they were the perfect aircraft for the job. Now Intruder missions could even reach into Germany itself.

In particular, Mosquitos hunted German bombers returning to their home bases who were particularly vulnerable as they came into land. The sheer number of kills achieved by Mosquito Intruders soon caught the Germans' attention and they began to set traps, using a bomber coming in to land as bait while a fighter or fighters circled above waiting to pounce on the Mosquito as it set up its attack. Mosquito pilots then in turn latched on to what the Luftwaffe was doing. A number of German aircraft were avoided and spared, precisely because their pilots seemed to be flying particularly badly. A number of trainee German pilots thus

ABOVE: Three de Havilland Mosquito FB Mark VI Series 2s of No. 487 Squadron RNZAF based at Hunsdon, Hertfordshire, flying in tight starboard echelon formation, with 500-lb MC bombs on fitted on underwing carriers

had lucky escapes…Mosquitos also launched night strikes against the German fighter bases, hoping to disrupt their ability to intercept RAF heavy bomber streams now flying to and from targets across Europe.

'Day Ranger' and 'Night Ranger' missions saw Mosquitos freed up to roam over a designated area, striking at any targets of opportunity. They proved formidable hunters.

FIGHTER BOMBER

The value of Intruder missions over Europe was quickly recognised and, to further the Mosquito's destructive capacity, the new fighter-bomber variant was eagerly awaited. It was designated the Mosquito FB VI and would become the most common Mosquito variant. 2,298 would be built.

Based on the F II, it would retain the same firepower as the fighter with its four machine guns and four cannons, but would have the added advantage of being able to carry two 500lb bombs in its bomb bay. (Later developments allowed for an extra 500lb of bombs, drop tanks or eight 60lb rockets to be fitted under the wings. For maritime operations, the FB VI could deploy mines and depth charges. For ground support, the aircraft was also capable of carrying smoke screen canisters). Powered by twin Merlin 21s or 25s, the Mk VI carried no airborne radar, as it was intended mostly for day use.

The prototype, HJ662/G, first flew on 1 June 1942. It was destroyed just a few weeks later when an engine failed on take-off and the plane ploughed into two parked Beaufighters. This, along with some confusion at the Air Ministry meant that the first production models would not become available until a distant February 1943.

THE PATHFINDERS

Initially no-one knew how effective or ineffective British bombing in the war was — until the publication of The Butt Report in August 1941. Studying film and photos of the aftermath of raids, it showed that Allied bomber crew reports were wildly inaccurate. Of the aircraft which reported hitting their target, only one in three on average got anywhere near five miles of their target. On nights with no moon to fly by, only 1 in 15 bombers came within five miles of their target. 49% of all bombs dropped were falling on open countryside. Someone joked that far more cows were being killed than Germans. A further, equally shocking report estimated that, to kill just one German on the ground, the RAF would have to drop 5 tons of bombs. They were losing one bomber for every ten tons.

By the end of 1941, Bomber Command was experiencing such heavy losses — and hitting so few targets to any effect — that the whole bomber effort was being called in question and missions began to decrease significantly. There was even talk of shutting it down and sharing out its resources between the army and the navy. Something had to change.

During the Blitz of 1940/41, the Luftwaffe had developed a tactic to get their bombers close to target by night. An elite squadron was assembled to fly ahead of the main force and illuminate the target with flares. The regular bombers following up would then home in on the illuminated area. Perhaps the RAF might do the same…

In August 1942, aircrew began to be transferred out of their squadrons (after clandestine interviews, usually down the pub) and into the newly formed Pathfinder Force (PFF) under the command of 32-year-old Australian Group Captain Don Bennett. Five squadrons of Pathfinders were originally established — one for each of the five bomber groups. Lancasters were the chosen aircraft for No.5 Group and 83 Squadron. Other groups had Mosquitos, Stirlings, Halifaxes and Wellingtons assigned to them. Crews were given a temporary raise in rank and pay. From the start Bennett wanted just two aircraft type to serve as Pathfinders — The Lancaster and the Mosquito - but he was forced for use whatever could be made available to him. Bennett was an early proponent of the Mosquito having flown it on a number of occasions and vigorously defended its inclusion in Bomber Command against critics from the Air Ministry.

'They declared that the Mosquito had been tested thoroughly by the appropriate Establishments and found quite unsuitable, and indeed impossible to fly at night. At this, I raised an eyebrow and said that I was very sorry to hear that it was quite impossible to fly by night, as I had

ABOVE LEFT: 83 Squadron aircrew in front of their Lancaster R5868, Squadron Leader Shailendra Eknath Sukthankar, an Indian Navigator stands in the middle, 28 February 1942

ABOVE: The Pathfinder wings worn beneath the aircrew flying badge by members of Pathfinder Force

RIGHT: Australian Group Captain Don Bennett

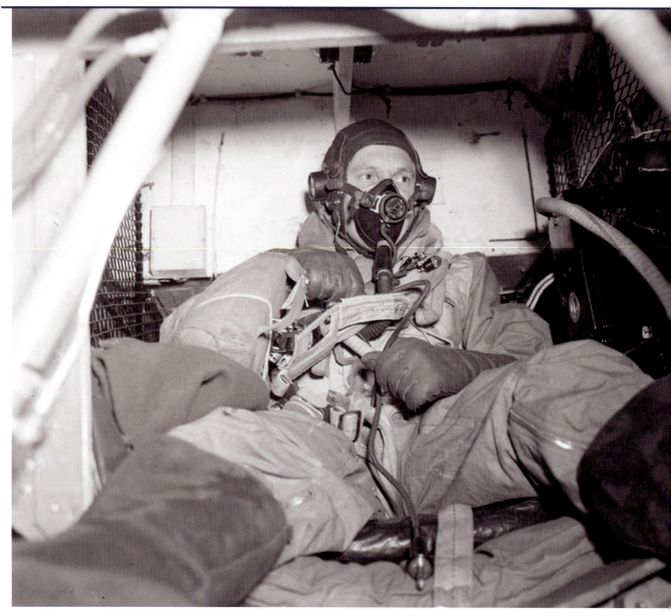

been doing so regularly during the past week and had found nothing wrong. There was a deadly silence. I got my Mosquitos.' - Group Captain Don Bennett.

The Mosquito was about to find another role in which it would truly excel, marking targets at any altitude from less than 100 feet to six miles up.

BUILDING THE MOSQUITO DOWN UNDER

With the Mosquito desperately needed for operations in the Far East after Pearl Harbour, it was decided to build the aircraft at the de Havilland Factory in Bankstown, near Sydney, Australia. Plans, jigs and sample materials began to be shipped out from Britain in the summer of 1942. A

ABOVE: A passenger travelling in the bomb bay of a de Havilland Mosquito of BOAC, on the fast freight service between Leuchars, Fife and Stockholm, Sweden

sample Mosquito was also shipped out to familiarise all with the aircraft and this first flew in Australia in December 1942. The first aircraft came off the production line in July 1943 and the Mosquito began service with the RAAF in March 1944. 108 Mosquitos would be produced for RAAF operations before the end of the war. Post-war production took the tally of Australian Mosquitos to 212.

The Bankstown plant specialised in producing fighter-bomber variants. Of these, a half dozen were converted for photoreconnaissance duties and the plant also built 17 dedicated PR versions. Australian fighter-bombers were designated FB 40 and were very similar to the FB VI, but built using Packard-Merlin 31/33 engines.

'A BOMBER IN CIVVIES'

On 6 August 1942, Mosquitos began to be used to deliver Foreign Office communiques to and from neutral Sweden on behalf of BOAC. The first Mosquito to be used — from 105 Squadron - was stripped of all military markings and the pilot and observer told to wear civilian suits, but still had to face a ferocious gauntlet of marauding German fighters over the North Sea and the Skagerrak. The Mosquito now found another new role as *'a bomber in civvies'*.

After the complete success of the first mission, a regular night service was started from 4 February 1943 out of Leuchars in Scotland bound for Bromma airport in Stockholm. Flight time was three hours each way. A small number of BOAC civilian airmen were allowed to take the Mosquito up and over to Stockholm after receiving training. After the initial test run, a Mosquito B IV was especially converted for the task, with extra fuel tanks stowed in the bomb bay. The new aircraft was designated G-AGJV and retained camouflage to help it evade enemy interceptors. Six more unarmed Mosquito bomber conversions were supplied to BOAC between April and May 1943. These comprised both converted B IV's as well as FB VIs.

In mid-May 1943, a BOAC Mosquito was converted to carry a passenger for the first time, tucked away uncomfortably in what remained of the bomb bay next to the extra fuel tanks. The passenger who would lie down on a mattress, had to wear a safety harness, flight suit, oxygen mask, parachute and life jacket. They had access to a reading lamp and were usually supplied with a book and a packed lunch. They could also communicate with the crew via an intercom. The first two passengers were whisked across to Stockholm in a pair of Mosquitos to negotiate buying Sweden's entire output of ball bearings for the war effort. The effort was successful and, in future, Mosquitos would be used to carry up to 1,300lb of ball bearings back to Britain in a single run. The service was also used to carry VIPs from Sweden into Britain as well as to repatriate any RAF aircrew who had been shot down but had managed to reach neutral Sweden. A journalist for the Daily Telegraph, who had experienced the journey himself wrote:

> **'Riding across the North Sea is like squeezing into a tiny ice box and crouching there stiffly for several hours...'**

The danger the Mosquitos on the service faced was very real. Enemy fighter numbers increased as did the number of anti-aircraft guns en route as the Germans realised the importance of the run. As early as 22 April 1943, a BOAC Mosquito was caught and shot up by an Fw 190, and was forced to make a belly landing at Stockholm. On 17 August a further Mosquito was lost after hitting high ground on the run back to Leuchars and on 25 October Mosquito G-AGGG reported engine failure. It struggled to reach Leuchars, but came down just a mile short of the runway, killing both crewmen and their passenger.

Mosquitos were to be used as couriers for a number of important conferences in future years of the war. In 1944, a Mosquito PR aircraft made a four hour run to bring documents for the Moscow Conference and, during 1945 couriered documents for both the Yalta and Potsdam Conferences.

OBOE

Oboe was an ingenious attempt to make bombing raids more accurate in what was becoming ever more a technological battle. Developed by A H Reeves & F E Jones, it was called Oboe because of the distinctive noise it made — a sound that won Oboe-equipped aircraft the nickname of 'Musical Mosquitos'. An aircraft fitted with Oboe flew along a beam provided by a ground station (codenamed 'Cat') back in England. At the same time, another beam transmitted by a second, 'Mouse' station around 100 miles away would focus on the target. When the two beams crossed, the bombers dropped their payloads.

Oboe came with drawbacks. Firstly, it had a maximum range of 300 miles. This was adequate for bombers hitting German industry in the Ruhr, but it meant that it could not provide help on missions of greater range, such as attacks on Berlin to the east. There were only two stations in the whole of Britain to begin with and the entire two station system could only handle a dozen bombers every hour. To get the best accuracy from Oboe, planes had to fly straight and level for several minutes right over the target, making them particularly vulnerable to searchlights and flak. Because of the strict limits on its aircraft handling capabilities, it was assigned just to a Pathfinder aircraft, usually a Mosquito.

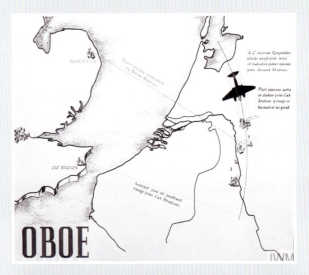

RIGHT TOP: The Telecommunications Research Establishment (TRE) at Malvern in Worcestershire where the system was developed in 1942

RIGHT MIDDLE: An illustration of Oboe being used

RIGHT BOTTOM: The left side of this image shows an Oboe navigation console. The two CRTs, some of the largest built during that era, were used for gross and fine distance measurement

The Mosquito was the ideal aircraft to use the system. It was the only bomber capable to reaching the height necessary to receive signals over Germany. This was identified by the Pathfinder Force in the summer of 1942, further cementing the Mosquito's role as an important part of future Pathfinder operations.

The Mosquitos of 109 Squadron at Wyton trialled the use of Oboe, the first set being installed on board B DK100 on 21 July 1942. Eight more Mosquitos were converted shortly after. On 20-21 December, Oboe had its first 'trial by fire' when it was used to guide six Mosquitos to their target — a power station at Lutterade in the Netherlands, which was right up against the German border. The raid was conducted at night. Unfortunately, three of the Oboe sets failed, and the remaining three guided their Mosquitos to a spot just under a mile off target.

On New Year's Eve 1942, two Mosquitos from 109 flew the first Oboe-led Pathfinder mission in conjunction with eight Lancaster heavies. The target was Dusseldorf, and the Mosquitos marked it with parachute flares before the Lancasters unleashed their payloads. Other Mosquitos from 109 were up the same night, using Oboe to find and bomb the German night fighter airbase at Florennes in Belgium.

Tests continued through into January 1943, mainly against power stations and blast furnaces, by which time Mosquitos were achieving 80-90% accuracy in their aim. 109 Squadron were then to see almost constant employment as Oboe-equipped Pathfinders for the Heavies attacking Germany's industrial heartland in the Ruhr. During this time it began to convert to Mosquito IXs.

DIVIDED OPINIONS

The Mosquito still divided opinion.

Pilots and navigators with few exceptions loved the aircraft and thought it a great improvement on whatever else they had flown in the war. Ground crews had taken

ABOVE: Portrait of Air Marshal Sir Philip Joubert

more convincing. They tended to be of an age where they believed any decent warplane should be made of metal and that a wooden design was a throwback to the days of the Great War. They were however slowly being won over when they saw for themselves just how much battle damage the Mosquito could take and still make it home.

The higher echelons of the RAF were another matter entirely. Many had harboured severe doubts about the Mosquito since its inception. They still balked at a wooden bomber with no defensive weapons — not even a decent

ABOVE: T12.8-cm-Flak on a flak tower

turret. When the numbers were crunched, it was realised that the Mosquito was suffering worse losses than the disastrous Blenheim in the early years of the war. It seemed a powerful argument to discontinue the aircraft. In early December 1942, the Chief of the Air Staff received an Air Ministry Directive ordering that the Mosquito be relieved of all bomber duties.

There were other voices of course, among them the head of RAF Coastal Command Sir Philip Joubert. He had employed what few Mosquitos he could get on long range photographic reconnaissance duties and quickly discovered that one Mosquito could do the work of at least two Spitfires. He wanted more Mosquitos — and was constantly frustrated that he couldn't get his hands on them.

Among the Mosquitos most ardent sceptics was the head of Bomber Command himself — Air Marshall Sir Arthur Harris. He had just spent most of 1942 trying out the Avro Lancaster and deciding that it was the most splendid thing and just what he needed. A well-performing four engine heavy, in formations of sufficient size it was capable of delivering a crushing blow to any German city. Harris didn't need any other aircraft in his arsenal, especially not one with a greatly smaller bombload. He didn't want the unarmed bomber — or the new fighter-bomber variant that was currently in production. He wanted muscle. He wanted heavyweights.

What Harris and his fellow critics failed to understand was that the Mosquito was proving a different kind of aircraft for a different kind of mission. It could attack specific targets with quite some precision and do it in daylight — an important consideration when many targets were in friendly countries occupied by the enemy.

It often enjoyed the element of surprise, being so fast and racing across the sea barely above the waves and below German radar. Flak batteries would have little or no advanced warning of its approach and it would be gone before the gun batteries were made ready. Crew joked that the main threat to the Mosquito en route were high cresting waves and unlucky sea gulls.

The heavies were imprecise weapons of mass destruction, far more suited to blitzing a city than a single factory or building. They were unsubtle, but then so was Harris. Harris was a man renowned for never changing his mind — but then something happened that finally helped him to realise the true potential of the Mosquito…

BELOW: RAF Air Chief Marshal Sir Arthur Harris

NORWEGIAN WOOD

Vidkun Quisling was the head of the fascists in Norway when the Germans invaded on 9 April 1940 and had supplied the Nazis with top secret defence information which he was privy to as a politician. He led a coup attempt as the Germans stormed in, and his failure to seize power left the Germans singularly unimpressed with him. Still, by the start of 1942 Hitler had warmed to his persistent devotion to National Socialism and appointed him as Prime Minister of Norway at the head of a puppet regime. His very name would become a byword for collaboration with the enemy.

On 25 September 1942, four Mosquito B IVs from 105 Squadron went after him.

It was discovered that Quisling was due to make a speech at a Nazi rally in Oslo that he himself had organised for his masters. It would be held inside the Gestapo headquarters at the Victoria Terrasse building, where the Nazi's main torture chambers were housed, along with important Gestapo files. It was just too tempting a target to ignore — but it would need pinpoint precision to hit just one building in the friendly Norwegian capital. A low level strike was decided upon, led by Squadron leader George Parry and his navigator Flying Officer Robbie Robson. In preparation, 105 Squadron aircraft relocated to Leuchars in Fife, Scotland to make the crossing to Oslo quicker. Still, the raid would be the longest ever attempted by a Mosquito at that time. Each aircraft was kitted out to carry two delayed-action 1000lb bombs.

On the day, the weather over Oslo was perfect. Attacking in two waves of two aircraft each, the Mosquitos raced in just 100 feet above the rooftops of the city. Three Fw 190s dived on them, blasting one of the Mosquitos and sending it plunging into a lake close by. A second took cannon fire in its starboard engine but was able to continue on with its bomb run. All three aircraft closed on Gestapo HQ, which stood out because of the peculiar red dome on its roof and then released their bombs. At least four of their bombs landed directly on target, but one or more failed to explode and the building suffered only limited damage. As they raced away again bound for a landing strip in the Shetlands, Norwegian civilians spontaneously saluted them by bursting into patriotic song. Sadly, at least 60 civilians were killed in the raid and several nearby buildings destroyed. Quisling survived the raid, cowering in a shelter. Later, he would furiously condemn the raid by *'RAF murder planes'*. It would take until 1945 for Quisling to receive justice in the form of a firing squad…

The raid was considered audacious enough that the RAF officially announced the existence of the Mosquito to the British Public through the BBC Home Service the day after. The Times joined in the fun with a headline announcing:

ABOVE: Mosquito B Mk.IV Series 2, DK338, built in September 1942 and delivered to 105 Squadron, becoming GB-O

LEFT: A depiction of a RAF de Havilland Mosquito bomber aircraft dropping bombs on Berlin

R.A.F. day raiders over Berlin's official quarter.

INTO ACTION

1942

ABOVE: This is the first picture released for publication of Britain's all-wooden Mosquito bomber, 21st December 1942

LEFT: Ministry of Aircraft Production poster, text reads; *'In a daring attack at very low level on the U-Boat yards at Flensburg, a Mosquito, skimming the roof-tops, struck a chimney-pot. It tore a huge hole nearly three feet wide in the fuselage near the wing root. That was right on the roof of Germany, by the Baltic coast, a very long journey home. The Mosquito made it without the slightest trouble, except that the crew felt a draught. but it was nothing like the draught the Flensburg Nazis felt.'*

BELOW: Diagram of Mosquito PR B & FB MKS Fuel system

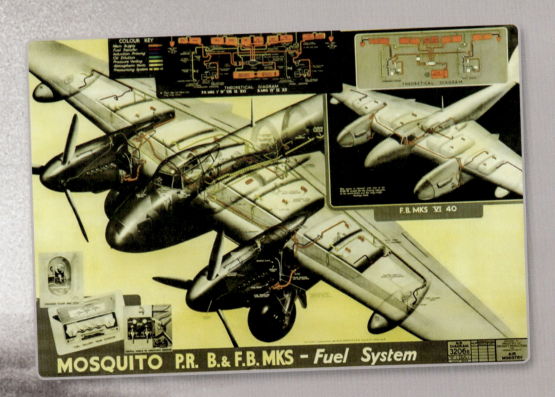

1943

> 'It makes me furious when I see the Mosquito. I turn green and yellow with envy. The British, who can afford aluminium better than we can, knock together a beautiful wooden aircraft that every piano factory over there is building....They have the geniuses and we have the nincompoops'
>
> Hermann Goering

SPOILING THE PARTY

30 January 1943 was a very special day for Nazi Germany. It marked the 10th anniversary of the Nazi Party seizing power. So of course the RAF planned to spoil the big day. At 11am, just as a radio presenter was opening celebrations and preparing to announce a speech by Reichsmarschall Hermann Goering live from the Hall of Honour in the Reich Air Ministry, listeners heard the unmistakeable sound of bombs falling and the radio station suddenly switched to classical music. Three Mosquito B IVs of 105 Squadron were over Berlin and their bombs were already dropping.

Sweeping across the German capital at 350 mph, they unleashed their payload at low level and darted away again. It was the first time that Berlin had been bombed in daylight and Goering's speech was delayed by an hour. At 4pm precisely, just as Minister of Propaganda Joseph Goebbels was due to make his speech, another three Mosquitos - this time from 139 Squadron - came in high over Berlin at 20,000 feet and unleashed another hail of bombs while Goebbels himself took to the shelters. One of the three was shot down by flak on the way home near Altengrabow - but Bomber Command had made its point.

Some flak popped up at us, close enough to be unpleasant, but not hitting the aircraft. It promised to be persistent, so we dived down, setting off for home.... It was late when we got our tea, but it was steak and chips, which were worth flying to Berlin for.' - Flight-Sergeant Peter McGeehan, RNZAF

The Germans knew that Mosquitos were responsible for both raids and that night infamous traitor 'Lord Haw-Haw' went on the radio to try and salvage some dignity. Thanks to Germany's glorious U-boat campaign, he sneered, Britain was so short of materials that they now had to make their planes out of wood…

THICK AND FAST

Following the successful raids on Berlin, Mosquito strikes were stepped up in the early months of 1943 against a wide variety of targets, with 105 and 139 bomber Squadrons in the thick of the action. On 5 February, Mosquitos from 139 flew against the armaments plant at Liege. On the 18th, they were over the railway depot at Tours and on 26 February they joined up with 105 Squadron to raid the U-boat pens at Rennes. In this last raid, the commander of 105 Squadron was killed when two Mosquitos collided in mid-air. Nine planes from 139 Squadron hit the molybdenum mines at Knaben in Norway on 3 March causing severe damage. Not one of their bombs fell outside the target area. They repeated the same feat while raiding the locomotive factory at Nantes on 23 March. 20 April saw 105 Squadron B IX

ABOVE: Wing Commander R W Reynolds (right), CO of No. 139 Squadron RAF, with his navigator, Flight Lieutenant E B Sismore, and a de Havilland Mosquito Mk IV 1943

LEFT: The Reich Air Ministry

Mosquitos over Berlin again by night to spoil Hitler's birthday party and to provide a much needed distraction to draw off German night fighters while the 'Heavies' went in over Stettin. They returned just over a month later to drop special demoralizing 'screamer bombs' on the capital.

While the Mosquito bomber crews were showing an ever-increasing rate of airmanship and accuracy, and were doing tasks no other aircraft was so suited to, there was still concern in some quarters about losses. The two squadrons had flown 193 operations between May 1942 and May 1943 — but it had cost them 48 losses. The promise of the imminent arrival of the new fighter-bomber variant helped to steel nerves.

EVER HIGHER

The seemingly charmed life of Mosquito PR versions could not last forever and better enemy interceptors were now posing a very serious threat to the unarmed aircraft. The solution decided upon was to make the Mosquito capable of even greater height. October 1942 saw the introduction of the PR VIII, which also benefitted from 50 gallon drop-tanks. This was quickly superseded by the PR IX which first flew in March 1943 and went into service with 540 Squadron in May. Its ceiling exceeded 33,000 feet. This eventually evolved into the PR XVI with its pressurised cockpit, of which 432 would be built.

WHERE AM I?

The new mark of photo reconnaissance Mosquito, the PR XVI, started to come off the production line in November 1943. However, it was a 'rush job' and so came with problems. Crews reported becoming disorientated at this new high altitude, leading them to sometimes forget what their target was or where they had been after their return. Cabin heating was also totally inadequate and the cockpit misted up or froze over with alarming regularity. These problems were not adequately solved until May 1944.

ACHTUNG MOSQUITO!

The Germans did not share any lingering British doubts about the Mosquito. They fully recognised the threat — to the extent that, in April 1943, Goering established what he called his 'Mosquito Net' two dedicated Fw190 units - Jagdgeschwader 25 and Jagdgeschwader 50 — specifically to counter the Mosquito. Despite Goering's assurance that any fighter pilot that shot down a Mosquito could count it as two 'kills', it is believed that not one of these elite interceptors shot down a single Mosquito. Later in the war, the Germans would try to develop their own 'Mosquito Hunter', the Focke Wulf Ta 154 'Moskito', but by then the damage had been done.

FB MK. VI - THE FIGHTER-BOMBER ENTERS SERVICE

The long anticipated fighter-bomber Mosquito variant finally came off the production line in February 1943. It was quickly pressed into action for daylight low level precision strikes. Fully armed with cannon and machine guns, it could now fight back against enemy interceptors and even AA ground positions. Eventually, 2,289 fighter-bomber Mosquitos would be built.

The first machines available, powered by Merlin 25s to increase speed at low level, were supplied during May 1943 to three dedicated Intruder/ Ranger squadrons — 418 (Canadian), 605 and 23 Squadrons, the latter of which was stationed on Malta. 23 Squadron fighter-bombers would now be capable of ranging as far as the Balkans to strike at enemy targets. The new fighter-bombers proved particularly suited for Ranger and Intruder missions and continued to dominate in that role until war's end.

In June 1943, the Allies started amalgamating Squadrons into 2 TAF (Tactical Air Force), with a view to supporting the invasion of Europe in the following year. This would later evolve into the Allied Expeditionary Air Force. Other joined ADGB — the Air Defence of Great Britain.

Two Dominion Squadrons — 464 and 487 Squadrons - were converted from flying Venturas to Mosquito FB VIs on 21 August 1943. 487 Squadron recorded in their ops book their delight at receiving their Mosquitos:

'The Mossies that arrived last night have been exercised fairly hard all day in glorious weather. It is a pretty aircraft. The Squadron is generally as pleased as a child with a new toy…all anybody talks about here is Mosquitos.'

They were joined at their new base at Sculthorpe by 21 Squadron who were also given FB VIs. By September, the three Squadrons could claim 70 Mosquitos between them. They now comprised 140 Wing as part of 2 Group. 2 Group was under the command of Air Vice Marshal Basil Embry, a true Mosquito enthusiast who rapidly sought to get rid of his less able aircraft - Bostons and Venturas - and standardize on just two aircraft in the Group — the Mitchell and the Mosquito. Squadrons under his command were, on receipt of their new Mosquitos, said to be '*Basilized*'.

Command of 140 Wing fell to Group Captain Charles Pickard, who was something of a celebrity having starred in the propaganda film '*Target For Tonight*', then flying Wellingtons. He was also one of Bomber Command's most decorated officers.

ABOVE: RAF Mosquitos of No. 4 Squadron

BELOW: Geoffrey de Havilland with his two sons, Geoffrey and Peter

ABOVE: Building Mosquito Aircraft at the de Havilland Factory in Hatfield

BELOW: Painting the roundel on the side of a Mosquito at the factory

140 Wing were given operational status on 2 October. Just a day later, 24 Mosquitos from the wing attacked the Chateau power stations near St. Nazaire in two waves, accompanied by 36 Bostons. The first wave roared in at treetop height, dropping 500lb bombs while the second completed a shallow dive from 2,000 feet to add to the devastation. Six Mosquitos were damaged by fierce anti-aircraft fire, but all returned home. Pickard himself had to return on one engine. However, six Bostons were also lost to ack-ack. The second raid carried out by 24 aircraft from 464 and 467 was a near disaster. Foul weather kept most of the Mosquitos from locating their targets and four aircraft were lost. Most tragic of all, alterations had been made to the cockpit of the Mosquitos which led to confusion between the intercom switch and the bomb release switch. When pilots in two of the four lost aircraft — all flying at treetop height - switched on their intercoms, they accidentally released their bombs directly below them and were consumed by the blast. None of the bombs had delayed fuses. A couple of Mosquitos, thoroughly lost but unwilling to bring their bombs home, looked for targets of opportunity and hit factory plants and canal barges on the way back.

As more Mosquito FB VIs became available, a second wing was formed. 138 Wing, based at Lasham, was established on 14 October, first comprising 613 Squadron who were later joined by 107 Squadron and 305 Polish Squadron. They became operational in December 1943. Meanwhile Day Rangers of 21 Squadron first flew their new FB VIs into battle on 25 November against a transformer station at Vannes. 464 Squadron in particular were given responsibilities as night intruders as part of Operation Flowers, bombing enemy airfields and stalking the skies above them for 'trade'.

BELOW: De Havilland Mosquito B.XVIs, including the Percival-built PF563, closest to the camera

THE MALTA PIRATES

In the closing days of 1942, 23 Squadron — having previously been on Intruder duties over Europe — was moved to Malta in the Mediterranean. They immediately found themselves very busy, flying over 180 Intruder sorties during their first month on the island. Those sorties included devastating Axis shipping in the Mediterranean as well as attacking enemy airfields and strafing trains and road traffic in North Africa, Sicily and mainland Italy. They could claim 200 trains destroyed by May 1943, as well as 30 enemy planes brought down for the loss of seven Mosquitos. They quickly gained the nickname '*The Pirates of Malta.*' In July 1943, 23 Squadron was joined by 256 Squadron, again equipped with old Mosquitos no longer required for the European theatre since the arrival of the new fighter-bomber types. 23 Squadron however started receiving new VIs from the start of July, flying their first fighter-bomber mission just over two weeks later when Axis airfields in the vicinity of Rome were shot up.

Although the Mosquito had always been intended to operate in hot climates, in reality it suffered in Malta, most notably from overheating. There was also a desperate short of planes and spare parts, which left ground crews to come up with their own innovative if unorthodox solutions. Damaged Mosquitos on Malta were patched up with anything that came to hand, from wood stripped from cigar boxes and tea chests to coffins.

Following Italy's surrender, the 'Pirates' left Malta and 23 Squadron Mosquitos operated from Italian bases at Sigonella and Alghero, mostly as Night Intruders. Their tally of trains 'busted' increased to 331. From early April they were switched to Day Ranger missions before being reassigned to England in June where they flew out of Little Snoring. Now the squadron flew support for the 'Heavies'

ABOVE RIGHT: This spectacular series of six stills was taken from a de Havilland Mosquito NF Mk. II while intercepting a Ju 88 over the Bay of Biscay during bad weather.

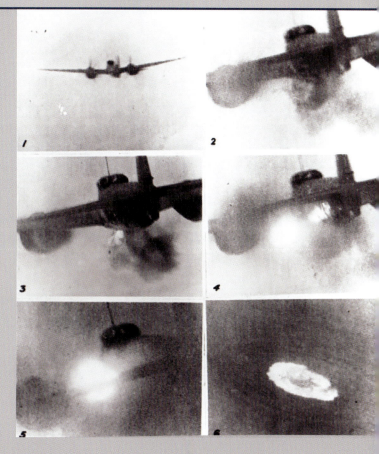

out over Europe until finally in April 1945 they were tasked with dropping incendiaries on German airfields.

WAR IN THE BAY OF BISCAY

'Bloody Biscay' well earned its nickname. As the war progressed, Allied Merchant shipping on the Atlantic convoys increasingly fell prey to marauding U-Boats.

In March 1943, the Mosquito found yet another new role — as a U-Boat hunter. Its extended range made it perfect for the task, but its guns and 20mm cannon were all but ineffective against the steel hull of a U-boat caught on the surface. The Ministry of Aircraft Production then came up with the idea of mounting what was effectively an artillery piece onto the Mosquito Fighter-Bomber. The 6lb artillery piece to be fitted became known as 'The Molins Gun' or just 'The M-Gun', replacing the 20mm cannon.

A detachment from 618 Mosquito Squadron based In

ABOVE: Mosquito F Mk.II in India circa 1943

Predannack in Cornwall, were chosen to fly the newly designated FB XVIII — now known as the 'Tsetse' - and began anti-U-boat operations in the Bay of Biscay in October 1943, by which time the detachment had amalgamated with 248 Squadron. The first operation was a tragic failure, with a Mosquito lost to anti-aircraft fire from gunships escorting a U-boat in the bay. Both crew died. Just three days later, another 618 Squadron managed to severely damage a different U-Boat caught on the surface heading for its base at Brest. At first, the Tsetses were escorted everywhere by 248 Squadron Beaufighters but these were replaced with Mosquito FB. VIs by December.

The Kriegsmarine responded to the new threat by ordering their captains to stay on the surface and duel it out with the Tsetses using their own 20mm cannon. They discovered in short order that this would result in much less than a fair fight and by December, U-Boat crews were restricted to travelling on the surface only under cover of darkness. Admiral Doenitz himself ordered;

Although U-boats were intended to be their primary prey, Tsetses also flew missions against more conventional shipping. On 10 March 1944, two Tsetses with their Mk VI escorts met ten Ju88s over Biscay. The Tsetses attacked a U-Boat and an escort destroyer before joining in the fight with the Ju88s. Incredibly they managed to shoot down a Ju 88 with a shot from their 6lb-er gun.

The success of the Tsetses resulted in a second coastal strike squadron — 235 in Scotland — been set up and directed against enemy shipping off occupied Europe in June 1944 before switching to strike duties off the coast of Norway.

Only around 28 Tsetse Mosquitos were ever built, mainly because rockets became available to sling under the wings of regular Mosquitos and were believed to have an even more devastating effect against U-Boats and surface ships. A Tsetse never succeeded in sinking a U-Boat by itself by war's end, but it did damage a number and succeeded in forcing severe restrictions on German U-Boat movements and deployment.

> **'Owing to damage caused by enemy aircraft mounting heavy calibre guns, surface passage will only take place during the hours of darkness'**

AT WAR IN THE FAR EAST

Mosquitos had first appeared in the Far East theatre in April 1943, with the arrival of six Mosquitos for 27 Squadron to test. These were subsequently transferred to 681 Photo Reconnaissance Squadron based at Dum-Dum in India in the summer of 1943. They flew a number of sorties over Burma and Siam (Thailand), paying particular attention to Japanese-held ports and railways before the squadron decided to standardise on Spitfires. The Mosquito detachment from 681 then became part of the newly established 684 Photoreconnaissance Squadron. Now their mix of Mosquito PRG IIs and FB VIs — plus two newly-arrived Mosquito PR IXs were used in particular for long range missions (sometimes in excess of eight and a half hours) until the end of the war. The squadron lost its first Mosquito over Rangoon on 2 November 1943. Two more would be lost before the end of the year, one ominously due to structural failure. Ironically, Mosquitos did not like tropical weather.

When Major Hereward de Havilland arrived on an inspection tour, he was left horrified by the state of the Mosquitos he found but, such was the enthusiasm for the aircraft, they were still being flown. His reminders about how a Mosquito should be properly maintained — even in tropical conditions — led to mild amusement behind his back. In the end he was forced to buy a log saw and start sawing the wing off a damaged Mosquito to let ground crews know he was serious. He even threatened to cut off the wings of every single Mosquito still in service if he wasn't taken seriously. After that, much more attention was paid by everyone concerned to successfully 'tropicalizing' the aircraft.

MORE MOSQUITOS FOR THE PATHFINDERS

109 remained the sole Mosquito Squadron in the Pathfinders force for almost a year. It had proven the aircraft was well suited to the job, perhaps uniquely so, but it wasn't until June 1943 that a second Mosquito squadron

ABOVE: Production H2S radar scope unit as flown during WWII

BELOW: Large areas like the Zuiderzee make excellent targets for the H2S. The resolution of the system is evident in the appearance of the Afsluitdijk (labelled "dam"), which is about 90 metres (300 ft) across'

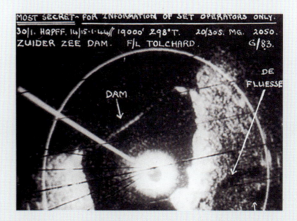

— No 105 — joined the PFF. No 139 became the third PFF Mosquito squadron a month later.

The three Mosquito squadrons combined Pathfinder operations with bombing missions of their own as part of the Light Night Striking Force.

THE LIGHT NIGHT STRIKING FORCE

The Light Night Striking Force (LNSF) was established in 8 Group in recognition of the unique contribution the Mosquito was making to the RAF Pathfinder force. (Bennett preferred to call it the Fast Night Striking Force but once again was overruled.)

It initially comprised the three Mosquito Pathfinder Squadrons — 109, 105 and 139 — but would grow as more Mosquitos became available. Those still flying the unarmed bomber version, like 105 and 109 Squadrons, were switched to night missions as of 1 June 1943. As a direct result, losses amongst these Mosquito Squadrons dropped to 1.75% of sorties flown.

109 Squadron, having pioneered the successful use of Oboe and having now been reequipped with B IXs, along with 105 Squadron were usually assigned Pathfinder target marking duties while 139 flew 'nuisance raids' to harass and confuse the enemy. Their 'nuisance raids' while hardly causing mass destruction, provided a valuable distraction to lure German attention away from the giant Heavy raids. A typical mission, flown by 139 Squadron in their Mk XIs on 3 October, saw the Squadron attack Hanover as a diversion while the 'real' raid centred on Kassel. 139 succeeded in drawing away a large number of German night fighters, which they outraced, before scattering 'Window' to blind radar and then marked their own target with flares. Although the raid was officially just a diversion, the Mosquitos each carried four 500lb bombs in their bays as well as two more under each wing — and 'spoof target' or not, all were dropped in anger on Hanover.

Towards the end of the year, a slight improvement in the availability of Mosquitos saw the formation of 627 Squadron and then 692 Squadron using older Mk. IVs, while 139 Squadron were rewarded with Canadian-built B XX variants. On 2 December, they took them out to Berlin, attacking in three waves and delivering 'Window' to blind radar before dropping marker flares and then their bomb loads. Four Mosquitos from 627 Squadron also got in on the action, dropping bombs on 139's marker flares. 109 Squadron began to receive pressurised XVIs for high altitude work from early December 1943. Later 139 would be switched away from nuisance raids to actually become the foremost Pathfinder marking squadron in 1944, benefitting from the use of the new H2S radar system. The LNSF would also take to conducting 'Siren' raids — bombing several different targets during a single sortie.

During the war, Mosquitos of the LNSF would fly 27,239 sorties for the loss of just under 200 aircraft in total.

BELOW: British propaganda leaflet dropped over Essen (Germany) after an RAF bombing raid in March 1943. The main title says "Fortress Europe has no roof". Imperial War Museum, London

NIGHT SHIFT WITH THE HEAVIES

It was during 1943 that the Mosquito truly proved its worth to even its most ardent critics within Bomber Command, from strikes against the Ruhr through the devastating of Hamburg to the ferocious mass attacks on Berlin itself during the latter part of the year. It was everywhere — and doing everything.

Mosquitos flew ahead of the heavies to mark their targets as part of its Pathfinder role of course, but also flew to provide advanced weather reports (referred to as 'PAMPA' missions) and PR photographs of forthcoming targets, to provide diversionary strikes, and to attack enemy airfields. Mosquitos confused radar with 'Window' and often carried the high level electronic measures and counter measures required to fight an increasingly technological fight. New, better onboard radar was fitted. There was 'Monica' — a rearward facing radar to warn of an enemy lining up for attack; Serrate which allowed Mosquitos to home in on German airborne radar signals and hunt enemy aircraft from as much as 100 miles away. 'Boozer' helped Mosquitos identify enemy radar stations. These could then be jammed using technology codenamed 'Dina' and 'Piperack'. Perfectos could read the identification equipment on board German fighters. Mosquitos could also use Gee-H and H2S navigation and target-finding radar to improve their Pathfinder roles, or control an entire raid by acting as a 'Master Bomber'.

Night fighters such as I41 Squadron flew either side of 'Heavy' bomber streams on 'bomber support' duties hunting enemy night interceptors at high altitude with airborne radar dogfighting. This became jokingly known as 'Midnight Murder'. 278 Nazi night fighters would be claimed by Mosquitos during the course of the war and it was said that many German pilots suffered from 'Moskitoschreck' (literally: 'Mosquito Terror').

And of course, PR Mosquitos would then return to the targets to gain photographic evidence of the damage done the previous night.

BELOW: Hamburg after an aerial bombardment during Operation Gomorrah, which started in the night of July 25, 1943, when 791 bombers of the British Royal Air Force (RAF) attacked the city

ABOVE: Workers fitting out the two half sections of the fuselage of a de Havilland DH98 Mosquito twin-engined multirole fighter-bomber aircraft during construction of the aircraft for service with the Royal Air Force circa October 1943

ABOVE: RAF electricians testing and charging aircraft batteries These three are working at Ford in May 1943. The fighter station's sole resident squadron at this date was No 256, operating with Beaufighters and about to re-equip with Mosquitos

A CHANGE OF HEART

And so it was too that the usually unswervable Harris had a complete change of heart over the Mosquito. He had gone from a major critic to an avowed enthusiast for the aircraft, and was greatly frustrated that he still could not get enough of the aircraft for Bomber Command. He hectored both Sir Charles Portal 'the Chief of the Air Staff' and Sir Wilfrid Freeman at the Ministry of Aircraft Production to increase the numbers coming off the production line, but the factories still could not meet demand. Canadian production alone increased from 90 Mosquitos in 1943 to 419 during 1944, but it was still nowhere near enough.

Major Hereward de Havilland summed up Harris's change of heart saying:

'Even the C-i-C of Bomber Command knows of (the Mosquito's) existence, but this is mainly due to its activities as Pathfinder for the heavies…Air Marshal Harris told me that he had, quite frankly, been surprised at the success Mosquitos have had on low-level attacks (but)… for Pathfinding which, he stated, will become the most important of all duties, the Mosquito is indispensable.'

5 GROUP – NEW TACTICS

In mid-1943, a furious and protracted row broke out between Air Vice-Marshal Bennett of 8 Group and Air Vice-Marshal Ralph Cochrane of 5 Group. Cochrane believed that target-marking from high altitudes was far less accurate than performing the task from relatively low altitudes. Bennett disagreed, saying far more Pathfinders would be shot down if they resumed low level missions. Cochrane decided that 5 Group would go its own way

ABOVE: Air Marshal Sir Arthur Harris (left) observes as Wing Commander Guy Gibson's crew is debriefed after No. 617 Squadron's raid on the Ruhr Dams, 17 May 1943. Debriefing of Wing Commander Guy Gibson's crew. Squadron Leader Townson, Intelligence Officer, questions, from left to right: Spafford, Taerum and Trevor-Roper. Pulford and Deering are partly hidden. Air Chief Marshal Sir Arthur Harris and the Hon Ralph A Cochrane, Air Officer Commanding the Group, observe

ABOVE: loading bombs onto a de Havilland Mosquito

and develop its own tactics. 617 'Dambusters' squadron started working up new low level tactics, and tested them out during a Lancaster attack on the Gnome & Rhône aircraft-engine factory at Limoges France, on 7 February 1944. The attack was a great success, with a Lancaster flown by Wing Commander Leonard Cheshire diving on the target from 3,000 feet and dropping his markers at just 500 feet off the ground. Cochrane seemed to have proved his point, but the experience left Cheshire convinced that flying a Mosquito would be a far better bet than a heavy Lancaster in future. He managed to purloin three for 617 Squadron and converted himself to Mosquitos, flying an FB VI to mark targets.

Bennett had many virtues but being a good loser was not one of them. His fight with Cochrane became so fierce and so public that Harris himself was forced to intervene. He took 627 Mosquito Squadron from Bennett's PFF along with two Lancaster PFF Squadrons and handed them over to Cochrane to use as he saw fit. 627 Squadron, it must be

said, had their doubts about Cochrane's new tactics. They were told to drop their markers from 1,000 feet but found lower altitude still led to even more accuracy. As a result, they began to return home covered in branches or — on at least one occasion — with a brick from the target building embedded in a wing.

ABOVE: Building Mosquito Aircraft at the de Havilland Factory in Hatfield, Hertfordshire, 1943 - Mrs Judd prepares strips of wood to tack over gauze inside the hull of a Mosquito aircraft

BELOW: A de Havilland Mosquito of No 456 Squadron, flying from Middle Wallop, Hampshire, Britain, 1943. The censor has scratched out the wing-tip antennae of the Airborne-Interceptor radar

SECRET MISSIONS

At the very end of 1943, 140 Wing were ordered to fly missions against the newly located V-1 Flying Bomb sites springing up in France and the Low Countries. These missions were conducted in secret, as the government feared the public would be panicked by new German 'terror' weapons. Hitting small targets often in coastal locations was something the Mosquito was well suited to, and they enjoyed some success in limiting — if not eliminating — the forthcoming threat. June 1944 would see the Mosquito redeployed to dual with the Vis — in flight.

ABOVE: Test pilot John de Havilland checking the flight log book with two fitters beside a Mosquito after a test flight at the de Havilland Factory in Hatfield, Hertfordshire, 1943

LEFT: Fitters making adjustments to the tailplane of Mosquito HJ728 at Hatfield, Hertfordshire, 1943

1944

'It's a death-or-glory show. If it succeeds it will be one of the most worthwhile ops of the war. If you never do anything else you can still count this as the finest job you could ever have done'

Group Captain Charles Pickard

OPERATION JERICHO

Starting in late 1943, a large number of members of the French Resistance were betrayed and arrested because of the information provided by collaborators. Some of those seized by the Gestapo even possessed vital knowledge about Allied top secret plans for D-Day. If they cracked under torture, months — or even years — of Allied planning might be ruined.

The prisoners — some 832 of them — were held in Amiens jail, located 75 miles north of Paris. There were plans by the resistance to launch an audacious ground attack on the prison to free their compatriots, but when this failed to materialise, other plans had to be put together. Now it would fall to RAF Mosquitos to launch a rescue attempt with an air raid that would become one of the most famous of the entire war.

The raid would require an ultra-low level bombing raid in broad daylight with pin-point precision — hazardous, but just the sort of attack the Mosquito had proven itself uniquely capable of. Designated Operation Jericho, the raid would be undertaken by six Mosquito fighter-bombers each from 487, 464 and 21 Squadrons, carrying four 500lb bombs per aircraft. Each squadron would also be provided with a squadron of Typhoon escorts and a further Mosquito PR 1 would accompany the raid to film the attack. The raid itself was planned for noon, when the guard would be

distracted by their lunch. The plan was for the first Mosquito Squadron in to blow up the outer perimeter wall and for the next squadron in to blow holes in the prison itself. The shock waves from their bombs, it was theorised, would spring open the locks of the prison cells. The prisoners would then flee through the holes in the walls and be whisked away to safety by members of the French resistance waiting beyond the outer perimeter, who would also supply them with fake identity cards, civilian clothes and getaway bicycles. The third squadron, held in reserve, was — if all else failed — to come in ten minutes later to bomb and flatten the prison and kill as many captives as they could.

The importance of the raid was obvious. Head of 2 Group and now promoted to Air Vice-Marshal, Basil Embry wanted to lead the raid himself, but he knew too much about plans for D-Day and was forbidden to go. Instead, Group Captain Charles Pickard, the CO of No. 140 Wing, was ordered to command the raid. Like Embry, he was very much a man who liked to be in the thick of the action.

> ## 'We have been informed that the prisoners would rather be killed by our bombs than by German bullets'
>
> Group Captain Charles Pickard

ABOVE: An airman of the 25th Bomb Group with a Mosquito (H, serial number MM 388)

LEFT: Group Captain Charles Pickard

29-year-old Yorkshireman Charles 'Pick' Pickard was an unmistakeable figure at Sculthorpe being a lanky 6 foot four, blonde and accompanied everywhere by an Old English Sheepdog called Ming. He was a night pilot by trade and had to undergo ten hours of special training before the raid to try and get him used to daylight low level ops.

The raid was planned for 17 February 1944 but low cloud and sleet over the Channel led to it being postponed until the following day when, hopefully, the weather might have improved. It didn't — but there was no option but to fly; the Nazis had planned mass executions in the prison for the day after and had already dug a mass grave. Because of the foul weather, navigators were keen to tie the flight course down to the fine detail. Pickard laughed them away saying:

'Bugger the course. Just follow me – you'll be all right'

When the 19 Mosquitos took off the following morning, they flew straight into fog and a ferocious snowstorm. Few of them had ever flown a mission in weather so bad, with cloud cover down to 100 feet. As one airman later recalled, '*It was like flying in a blancmange.*' There was little improvement until the lead Mosquito Squadron was two miles off the French coast, whereupon the Mosquitos suddenly found themselves in sunny skies with thick snow on the ground under them. Six Mosquitos had already had to turn back, due to becoming lost in the snowstorm,

RIGHT TOP: Four 500-lb MC bombs being loaded into a Mosquito FB.VI of 464 Squadron, RAF Hunsdon

RIGHT: Pilots of No. 161 (Special Duties) Squadron- Group Captain Percy Charles "Pick" Pickard (centre) with his sheepdog 'Ming' alongside Squadron Leader Hugh Verity (left) and Flight Lieutenant Peter Vaughan-Fowler (Right) in the garden area behind Tangmere cottage, 1943

engine failure or damage caused by ack-ack.

Ahead of them, the Mosquitos could see Fw 190 interceptors taking off from Glisy airstrip, and heading on a direct intercept. They were engaged by the Typhoon escorts almost immediately.

The Mosquitos raced in so low that their slipstream churned up the snow covering the ground below. Sweeping in from a height ranging from 50 feet to an incredible ten feet above the ground, the first bombers succeeded in breaching the outer walls of the prison. The prison itself was then bombed by Mosquitos flying at a height of 100 feet, bringing down the walls and destroying the German guardhouse.

'You could tell (the French) from the Germans - because every time a bomb went off, the Germans would dive to the ground, but the prisoners kept on running like hell.' — Mosquito crewman

Flying above at 500 feet, Pickard watched as prisoners began to stream out of the stricken prison and make for the breech in the outer walls. He was then bounced by two Fw190s. He managed to damage one with his machine guns and cannon, but the second shot his Mosquito's tail away, flipping Pickard's aircraft onto its back. He and his navigator, Flight Lieutenant John Broadley, both died in the resulting fiery crash.

With Pickard lost, it was the PR1 that broadcast the order 'Red *Daddy Red*' — the coded instruction to call off the strike by 21 Squadron which would have had them try to kill everyone inside the prison.

As the Mosquitos turned and raced for home, they flew straight into the wheeling, murderous dogfight between

BELOW: The New Zealand contribution to the raid on 18 February 1944 was six Mosquitos of no. 487 (NZ) Squadron, led by Wing Commander Irving Smith

LEFT T-B: Mosquitos SB-U and SB-V of 464 Squadron crossing the Channel towards Amiens. R487 Squadron Mosquitos over Amiens Prison as their bombs explode, showing the snow-covered buildings and landscape. A photo taken two days later shows damage to prison including a hole in the perimeter wall (right-of-centre)

the Fw 190s and the RAF Typhoons. Pickard's fate was not known to his men for several days, but Ming his Old English Sheepdog knew and collapsed and was desperately ill after the raid. A further Mosquito was lost to German anti-aircraft fire. The pilot survived but the navigator was killed when flak hit their cockpit. One Typhoon escort was also shot down, while the Germans lost several Fw 190s in the action.

The raid still remains controversial today. Of the 832 prisoners held at Amiens, only 255 managed to break out of the prison building. 100 fellow prisoners died in the bombing. As they ran, a number of escapees were mown down by machine guns and a further 182 were recaptured in short order. Three escapees found a successful hiding place in a brothel, where the Madame was also a member of the resistance and who hardly ever went anywhere without a clutch of hand grenades hidden about her ample person.

> ### '*Financing escapes with money the Nazis spend here is one of my greatest pleasures – the other is killing them*'
>
> **French brothel Madame**

Other prisoners escaped disguised as German guards or even as monks or a blind man with a white stick. Predictably, the Germans took brutal reprisals for the raid on the local civilian population.

GESTAPO KILLERS

With their ability to hit targets in the middle of friendly cities in ultra-low daylight raids, it's not surprising that Mosquitos became the aircraft of choice to attack Gestapo headquarters and prisons in occupied Europe on a number of occasions.

In one such raid, 613 Squadron Mosquito FB VIs blitzed the five storey Gestapo Headquarters in The Hague on 11 April 1944 with HE and incendiaries to considerable effect with no losses. The Air Ministry called it a *'brilliant attack'*. Another such raid on 31 October 1944 involved twenty-four Mosquitos (plus a camera plane) led by Group Captain Peter Wykeham-Barnes making a 1200 mile round trip from RAF Swanton Morley to destroy the Gestapo Headquarters on the campus of the University of Aarhus in Jutland, Denmark. Eight RAF (Polish) Mustangs flew escort. Air Vice Marshal Basil Embry defied orders which had again forbidden him to fly on the raid, posing as *'Wing Commander Smith'*. He carried fake papers, and even had the name tag on his flying suit altered for the occasion.

The target was regarded as particularly fraught with difficulties as the dormitories which housed the Gestapo offices were located between two hospitals. Sweeping in at tree top level just before noon, the Mosquitos — from 21, 464 and 487 Squadrons - attacked in four waves each comprising six aircraft while the Mustang escorts blazed away, suppressing the AA defences. Two captive members of the resistance escaped during the chaos. The Germans returned anti-aircraft fire which damaged just one Mosquito. Under escort, this Mosquito made it safely to neutral Sweden. On the way back, the squadrons shot up any Nazi targets of opportunity they could spot and even took the opportunity to return the salute given by a lone Danish farmer as they flew by. Post war, the RAF were to refer to the Aarhus Raid as the most successful operation of its type conducted during the conflict.

BELOW: Group Captain P G Wykeham-Barnes, while Officer Commanding No. 140 Wing at Hunsdon, Hertfordshire. He assumed command of 140 Wing in March 1944, to be followed by his final wartime appointment on the Air Staff of No. 2 Group of 2 TAF in December

A combination of HE and incendiaries were dropped on the dormitories, destroying them. It's believed that up to 200 Gestapo members were killed in the attack and vital Gestapo files were incinerated.

Less successful was 627 Squadron's attack on the Gestapo Headquarters in Oslo on New Year's Eve 1944. The building had previously been attacked by 105 Squadron in an attempt to kill the notorious Norwegian traitor Vidkun Quisling. Divided into two waves, the Mosquitos came in in broad daylight and at rooftop height and succeeded in hitting the building but not seriously enough to destroy it. Tragically a Norwegian city tram was also hit in the action and 44 civilians were killed. The raid did however have the positive effect of making the local Gestapo feel vulnerable having been attacked by Mosquitos twice and resulted in them moving elsewhere, temporarily disrupting their activities.

THE MOSQUITO IN USAAF

Approximately 200 Mosquitos served with USAAF in the latter part of the war.

USAAF began to fly Mosquitos on a significant scale in February 1944, when they were more plentifully available. The 25th Bomb Group of the 8th Air Force, based at Watton, first flew PR XVIs as part of the Group's reconnaissance and weather information role. The group flew over 70 Mosquitos supplied by the British under a Reverse Lease-Lend Agreement. Unusually, when flying what was called a 'Red Stocking' mission which involved talking to secret agents based in Europe, a third crew member was carried in the bomb bay to record their coded conversation via wireless signals. OSS operatives were also on occasion carried in the bomb bay who then parachuted out over Germany. Other roles for USAAF Mosquitos included to secret radar experiments.

Although the Mosquito mostly operated with bomber units, at least one American fighter squadron flew the aircraft. The 416 Night Fighter Squadron based in Pisa, Italy, flew its first op on 17 December 1944, and operated twelve Mosquito NF 30s for mainly ground attack missions. P-51s replaced them on 1 June 1945.

COOKIE AND FAT BELLIES

Modifications to the B IV to adapt it to carry the new 4000lb 'Cookie' Bomb had been completed as early as April 1943, but it was not used operationally until 1944. Mosquitos adapted to carry the bomb — dreamed up by R.E. Bishop - were known colloquially as 'Fat Bellies' and officially as the B IV Special. The new bombs were personally championed by Harris, who was a firm advocate of dropping as much raw destructive power as he could from every aircraft on every raid. A single Mosquito over a target could now deliver 4,000lb of pure destruction; an American B-17 on its early

RIGHT: Diagram of a 4,000-lb HC Mark I bomb

LEFT: B Mk.IV (modified) of No. 692 Squadron, showing bulged bomb bay doors to accommodate the 'Cookie'

BELOW: Armourers wheel a 4,000-lb HC bomb ('Cookie') for loading into a de Havilland Mosquito B Mark IV (modified) of No. 692 Squadron RAF at RAF Graveley, Huntingdonshire

missions could only manage 3,500lb. And a Mosquito, because of its speed and range, could fly against a target twice in a single night.

On 23 February 1944, 692 Squadron, part of the No.8 Group's Light Night Striking Force, had the distinction of supplying three Mosquito B IVs to drop 'Cookies' on a target in Germany. It was used against Dusseldorf. Soon after, Mosquitos dropped their first 'Cookies' on Berlin. Harris liked the sheer muscle and raw destructive power that Cookies gave to the Mosquito and the LNSF now mainly flying adapted B XVIs was sent on more and more 'Cookie' missions against Berlin and other targets. In 1945, Mosquitos would drop 2,959 'Cookies' on Germany. Berlin was the target on 170 of those raids.

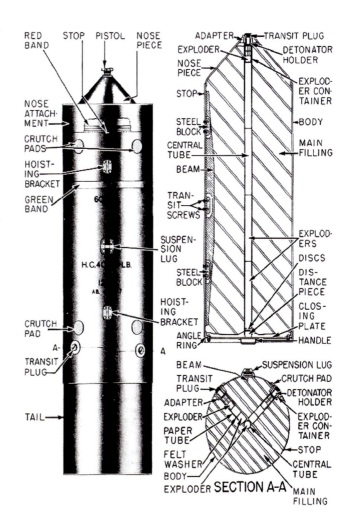

WAR IN THE FAR EAST 1944

February 1944 saw the arrival of nine pressurised PR IXs for high altitude reconnaissance ops over Asia and the surviving original Mosquitos were withdrawn. Reconnaissance became the Mosquito's recognised forte in the Far Eastern theatre, with long range recce missions lasting as much as nine hours over the jungles or vast stretches of seas. Even with extra fuel tanks, it was still impossible to cover the far reaches of the theatre. One solution used in Burma was for the Allied armies to build temporary airstrips right on their front lines where Mosquitos could land on their last drops of fuel and then for the crew to stay overnight with troops while the aircraft was refuelled before taking off again come morning.

On 20 October, a Mosquito from 82 Intruder Squadron suffered catastrophic structural failure, its starboard wing literally disintegrating and causing a fatal crash. All the Mosquito in India were immediately grounded. The Mosquito, it was found, still didn't fare well in tropical conditions. The searing temperatures and high humidity weakened the casein glue used on the airframe. Violent growths of white fungi would sprout on the fuselage and wings, while termites and White Ants found the Mosquito absolutely delicious and there were stories that almost an entire Mosquito could be consumed in a single orgiastic night by epicurean insects. The structural problems were at least partly resolved by the universal introduction of formaldehyde glue.

By the end of 1944 and the start of 1945, some Mosquitos started to be used for close air support for the advancing Allied army in Burma. Crews from different squadrons were converted onto Mosquito FBs with designated targets including Japanese held road, bridges, river traffic and railways.

BELOW: DH.98 Mosquito PR Mk XVI NS524 on Akyab Island, Burma, 1945

LEFT: Cover art for the August 1961 issue "Man's World" magazine with artwork by Gil Cohen, depicting a Mosquito bomber raid

CARRIER-BORNE MOSQUITOS

As if to prove the Mosquito's supreme versatility, in 1944 the aircraft began trials aboard the aircraft carrier *HMS Indefatigable* off the coast of Scotland. These would be the first attempts ever to successfully fly a two-engine aircraft off the deck of an aircraft carrier. The tests began on March 25, with Captain Eric 'Winkle' Brown — then the Royal Navy's Chief Test Pilot - at the controls of a modified FB VI. Brown personally rated the Mosquito very highly, later naming it as one of the three best RAF aircraft of the Second World War. The first three deck landings were conducted safely, but the fourth almost ended in disaster when the arrestor hook snapped. A specially strengthened hook was then produced at Hatfield for use with the Mosquito.

With trials successfully concluded, the Navy's specification N.15/44 resulted in the Mosquito TR 33, which was very much based on the FB VI. Significant differences on the carrier version included a reinforced fuselage, folding wings, four bladed propellers on the Merlin 25 engines and a newly designed undercarriage to stop the aircraft 'bouncing' on touch down. The four Browning MGs were replaced by radar, and the aircraft converted to be able to carry rocket racks as well as a torpedo or mine for anti-shipping operations. Fifty were built at Leavesden out of a total of 67 but none saw service with the Fleet Air Arm before the war ended.

Officially, the 'Sea Mosquito' entered service with the Fleet Air Arm in August 1946. Nine squadrons would eventually receive the 'Sea Mosquito', but it quickly became surpassed by other aircraft and was rapidly phased out again.

BELOW: Lieut Cdr Eric Melrose Brown, Naval Test Pilot who landed a de Havilland Sea Vampire Jet Aircraft on the flight deck of the British Aircraft Carrier HMS Ocean

PREPARATIONS FOR INVASION

In preparation for D-Day, the Allied Expeditionary Air Force pounded France for months with the intention of destroying the nation's transport infrastructure. Communication centres and ground defences were also targeted. Mosquito PRs played an invaluable role in gathering intelligence about everything from troop concentrations and clusters of armour to identifying targets and returning later to photograph the efficacy of raids.

Mosquito bombers and fighter-bombers struck at numerous targets by day and night, from low and high level. They blitzed trains, brought down bridges, collapsed tunnels and strafed troop convoys. Enemy airfields were another prime target, helping to weaken an already depleted Luftwaffe so that the Allies could enjoy air superiority come the invasion. Mosquito FB VIs from 107 Squadron were first switched from daylight raids on V-1 sites to night intruder missions against enemy airfields in April 1944. As the invasion got closer, they were then used to attack German road, rail and river networks. 109 Squadron were freed from their Oboe-related Pathfinder duties over Germany to launch daylight sorties against V-1 sites, enemy airstrips and road and rail networks. 305 Squadron, a Polish bomber unit, flew their FB VIs against V-1 sites at the start of 1944, but then concentrated on striking airfields, trail networks and big gun emplacements as invasion grew nearer. The Intruder Mosquitos of 418 Squadron RCAF persisted in Ranger patrols against railways and German airfields. They would let the personnel of each stricken airfield know who had attacked them by dropping a copy of The Edmonton Journal wrapped around a brick during a raid.

As part of 5 Group, 627 Mosquito Squadron put its distinctive low level target marking techniques to good effect. On 28 May a "bare handful of days before D-Day" they were up attacking German gun batteries on the Normandy coastline which such devastating effect that the German officer in charge reporting, '*The position has been hit with uncanny accuracy by the enemy air force*'.

In all the strikes, it was vital that the Germans couldn't tell the Allies' true area of interest. This meant hitting a lot of non-essential targets and almost right up until D-Day, four times the amount of bombs were dropped on the Pas de Calais area than around Normandy.

D-DAY

On the night before D-Day, eighteen aircraft from No. 21 Squadron flew strikes against German communications targets in the Caen area, just a few miles inland from the intended invasion beaches. They continued to attack communications targets in the area after the invasion, but were also sent against enemy troop concentrations. RCAF 464 Squadron Mosquitos left Gravesend on the night before the invasion to join in, strafing German rail and road targets. 109 Squadron were also up on the eve of D-Day, working as Pathfinders and concentrating on identifying heavy gun sites along the Normandy coast for the Heavies to follow. Also on the eve of D-Day, Mosquitos out of RAF Portreath in Cornwall responded to sightings of three 'Settier' class destroyers of the Kriegsmarine heading for positions in the Channel where they might pose a threat to the invasion fleet.

On D-Day itself, it seemed like Mosquitos were everywhere. 125 Fighter Squadron flew covering patrols in their XVII's over the invasion beaches along with the XVIIs of 219 Squadron, also a fighter unit. Mosquito fighter-bombers from 464 Squadron RAAF blitzed troop and armour concentrations plus bridges and railway targets just inland while 605 Squadron RAAF distinguished itself by shooting down the first enemy aircraft to be destroyed on D-Day. Converted B VIs were fitted with cameras to film the invasion, with a cameraman lying flat in the nose section with a 35mm film camera.

Mosquitos made one last, much appreciated contribution to D-Day. They flew over the beaches at day's end and dropped beer for the troops contained in their wing tanks.

BELOW: De Havilland Mosquito in D-Day Markings

THE BUZZ BOMB BLITZ

In mid-June 1944, Hitler unleashed the first of his V-weapons, the V-1, which was capable of flying without a pilot over the Channel and then crashing at random when its fuel expired detonating a ton of bombs stowed on board. In just a month, 2,754 'Buzz Bombs' rained down on Southern England and London. Although barrage balloons and anti-aircraft fire proved the most effective defences, RAF aircraft were also tasked with shooting then down in flight. V-1s were fast, travelling flat out at around 400mph, Mosquitos could just about catch them, so they joined with other high speed RAF fighters on 'Diver' patrols to chase them and blast them out of the skies and even on some occasions, flying next to then and disrupting them with turbulence.

The first successful aerial interception of a 'Buzz Bomb' was credited to a Mosquito FB VI flown by Flight Lieutenant J. G. Musgrave of 605 Squadron AAF out of RAF Manston on 14 -15 July. It was brought down 21 miles out of Dunkirk in total darkness. The Squadron would go to claim another 74 V1's which they managed to achieve while also carrying on with their assigned task of raiding German airfields in France.

By the beginning of September, the threat was almost over, thanks to the launch sites either being bombed into oblivion or overrun by Allied troops. RAF fighters in total accounted for 1,846 V-1s. Anti-aircraft guns and barrage balloons claimed another 2,109. In all, Mosquitos bagged an impressive tally of 623 'Buzz Bombs'. 418 Squadron RCAF was a specialist Intruder Squadron with a fearsome reputation for achieving kills by night and day. Pitched against the Flying Bombs during July and August 1944, they managed to catch and destroy no less than 123 V-1s. (They would later be recognised as the RCAF's highest scoring night fighter unit of World War Two). 96 squadron shot down 88 V-1s, destroying 24 of them in just a week in late June. 125 Squadron claimed 44 'kills' plus another 25 'probables'. 418 Squadron claimed 83 V-1s destroyed. 605 Squadron bagged 75 V-1s and 125 Squadron scored a total of 44 with another 25 'probables'.

BELOW: A German crew rolls out a V-1

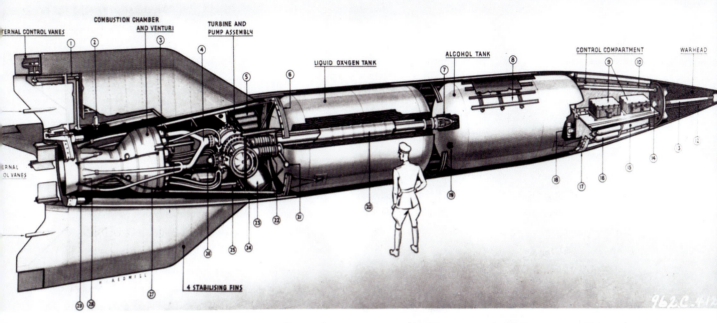

1 CHAIN DRIVE TO EXTERNAL CONTROL VALVE
2 ELECTRIC MOTOR
3 BURNER CUPS
4 ALCOHL SUPPLY FROM PUMP
5 AIR BOTTLES
6 REAR JOINT RING AND STRONG POINT FOR TRANSPORT
7 SERVO-OPERATED ALCOHOL OUTLET VALVE
8 ROCKET SHELL
9 RADIO EQUIPMENT
10 PIPE LEADING FROM ALCOHOL TANK TO WARHEAD
11 NOSE PROBABLY FITTED WITH NOSE SWITCH, OR OTHER DEVICE FOR OPERATING WARHEAD FUZE
12 CONDUIT CARRYING WIRES TO NOSE OF WARHEAD
13 CENTRAL EXPLODER TUBE
14 ELECTRIC FUZE FOR WARHEAD
15 PLYWOOD FRAME
16 NITROGEN BOTTLES
17 FRONT JOINT RING AND STRONG POINT FOR TRANSPORT
18 PITCH AND AZIMUTH GYROS
19 ALOCHOL FILLING POINT
20 DOUBLE WALLED ALCOHOL DELIVERY PIPE TO PUMP
21 OXYGEN FILLING POINT
22 CONCERTINA CONNECTIONS
23 HYDROGEN PEROXIDE TANK
24 TUBULAR FRAME HOLDING TURBINE AND PUMP ASSEMBLY
25 PERMANGANATE TANK (GAS GENERATOR UNIT BEHIND THIS TANK)
26 OXYGEN DISTRIBUTOR FROM PUMP
27 ALCOHOL PIPES FOR SUBSIDIARY COOLING
28 ALCOHOL INLET TO DOUBLE WALL
29 ELECTRO-HYDRAULIC SERVO MOTORS
30 AERIAL LEADS

ONWARDS AND UPWARDS

Mosquitos continued to be an essential part of the invasion in the weeks and months that followed, as the Allies broke out from the beach heads and surged northward. They flew — as might be expected of the Mosquito — in a wide variety of roles, expanding their Ranger and Intruder missions, while offering close air support to the men on the ground. Mosquito fighter bomber squadrons were given the task of running combat patrols over areas called 'Tennis Courts'. Each individual Mosquito was given its own hour over a particular 'Tennis Court' during which time it had absolute freedom to attack any road or rail transport it could find.

627 Squadron, for example, engaged in repeated raids in the days immediately after D-Day, flying on Montgomery's instructions to launch pin-point attacks on German troops and armour blocking the Canadian's advance around Caen. That same month they would fly low level marking missions to spotlight road and rail targets. Later, they would move on to concentrate on marking V-weapon related targets. 487 Squadron RNZAF took pride of place in attacking enemy rail and road networks in the first two months after D-Day. They also destroyed German barracks at Poitiers on 1 August and the SS headquarters at Vincey at the end of the month.

On the morning of 17 September 21 Squadron bombed targets in Nijmegen in support of Operation Market Garden — the ill-fated assault on Arnhem. 107 also bombed targets in support of the Arnhem operation but lost two aircraft in the process. They were ordered against German

ABOVE: A U.S. Army cut-away of the V-2

troop concentrations still on the 'wrong' side of the River Rhine and perhaps set some kind of record by blasting 29 trains in just one night — that of 1-2 October. To get closer to the action, like many Mosquito squadrons they were sent from England to a new base at Epinoy in France on 21 November 1944.

305 (Polish) bomber squadron concentrated on pin-point precision attacks after D-Day, notably flattening the German School of Sabotage as well as a large fuel depot. Later in the year, they would go after trains being used by the Germans as well as road convoys and canal barges. 613 Squadron AAF most notably flattened the SS barracks at Engletons, scoring at least twenty direct hits and doing a similar demolition job on German barracks close to Arnhem to support the paratrooper landings there.

PR missions didn't ease up either. From June to August 1944, 140 Squadron alone flew some 600 PR sorties. Of these, roughly one quarter were flown by night.

Harris was eager to get back to blitzing Germany itself and, whenever possible, he would send Mosquitos against targets in the Nazi heartland when they could be spared from supporting the Allied advance. 128 Squadron - a bomber unit - wasted no time when they received their first two Mosquito XXs on 8 September 1944. Within forty-eight hours, one of them was up and over Berlin dropping its payload. The next night, both new aircraft were up and bombing Berlin together — a

LEFT T-B: Mosquito NF Mk.II W4092 of 157 Squadron, January 1944, just visible is part of the aerial array for the A.I. Mk.IV near the wingtip. NF Mk.XIII of 256 Squadron, with the "bull nose", caught in the beam of a Chance light on the main runway at Foggia, Italy, before taking off on a night intruder sortie, 1944. Feeding the ammunition belt into a Browning machine gun. An FB Mk. VI NS898 of 613 Squadron, June 1944, shows full invasion stripes and is well weathered through operational use

raid they repeated on the 13 and 15 of the month. (By March 1945, 128 Squadron would have participated in 23 raids on Berlin — a number that rose to 65 by war's end.). 627 were also used against German targets and on 19 September, lent a Mosquito to Victoria Cross hero Guy Gibson of 'Dambusters Fame' for him to fly one last mission — because he was bored behind his desk. Acting as a 'master bomber' supervising a raid on Mönchengladbach, Germany, he was shot down and killed in circumstances that have never been clearly explained.

ABOVE: Wing Commander Guy Gibson (Right) and S/Ldr David Maltby (left) at RAF Scampton, on 22 July 1943

ROCKETS

In October 1944, plans to fit the Mosquito with eight underwing rockets finally came to fruition and they were quickly used both on ground support missions as well as against enemy targets of opportunity. The Mosquito could now carry a variety of different rockets ranging from 18lb high explosive shells right through to 60lb semi-armour piercing rockets with HE warheads. They proved simple, economical — and devastating (It has been claimed that the impact of a full 60lb rocket salvo fired from a Mosquito was a powerful as being on the receiving end of a broadside from a cruiser). Pilots lined up with their targets using their cannon and rockets were fired in a 20 degree dive. Normal procedure was to fire them off in pairs (one from each wing) or else to unleash a full salvo of eight against a single target.

By 1945, there were experiments to launch giant 1,050lb 'Uncle Tom' rockets from Mosquitos, but they were never to see service.

THE BANFF STRIKE WING

Banff (or Boyndie as it is known locally) was an air base built for RAF Coastal Command airfield on the coast of the Moray Firth in Scotland which became operational in April 1943. Originally used for flight training, in 1944 it was given over to operational units of what was to become known as the RAF Banff Strike Wing of Coastal Command. The first two Mosquito Squadrons stationed there were 144 and 404 Squadrons. More were to follow — 143, 235 and 248 and 333 (Norwegian) Squadrons — until the Wing reached full six squadron strength. They fought along with Beaufighter units which sometimes flew joint missions with

ABOVE: A de Havilland Mosquito on the ground with a RAE-Vickers rocket model in place below the fuselage

ABOVE: 25 lb, AP, No. 2 RP-3 aircraft rockets being mounted to a de Havilland Mosquito

the Mosquitos even after they moved on to RAF Dallachy.

From November 1944, the Mosquitos from Banff flew their own private war, mainly attacking enemy surface shipping in the North Sea or along the rugged coastlines of Norway. The aim was to starve the Nazis of supplies of Norwegian iron ore which they were increasingly reliant on to manufacture everything from tanks to aircraft to U-boats. Banff Strike Wing's brief however was wide enough to also see them attacking U-Boats (in which they enjoyed considerable success) as well as German airfields in Norway, defensive flak batteries and Axis shipping at harbour in Fjords.

The war waged by the Banff Strike Wing involved missions that were regarded as some of the most individually hazardous of the air war over Europe. They were usually conducted at ultra-low level and in daylight against well defended targets. The weather was often atrocious. The Squadrons paid the price. Over 80 crews were lost in action and rescue of any downed airmen proved exceptionally difficult due to distance, weather and ferocious German air defences. In return, their fighter-bombers wrecked a fearsome toll on the enemy with their cannon, machine guns and sets of solid armour-piercing rockets. In the Wing's first three months of operation, they sank almost 25,000 tons of enemy shipping.

LEFT: Smoke and flame erupt from a German Junkers Ju 88 torpedo-bomber as it crashes into the North Sea while Royal Air Force de Havilland Mosquitos of the Banff Strike Wing (144, 235, 248, 333 (Norwegian) Squadrons, RAF) circle overhead

BELOW: The German type XXI submarine U-2502 comes under cannon fire from a Royal Air Force de Havilland Mosquito FB Mark VI during an attack on four surfaced U-boats (U-251, U-320, U-2502, U-2335) and an M-class minsweeper escort (M403) in the Kattegat by 22 Mosquitos of the Banff Strike Wing

Norway was particularly well defended by the Luftwaffe and there were a number of occasions in which raids by the Banff Strike Wing descended into mass dogfights. On Boxing Day, 1944, a raid on Lervik Harbour by twelve Mosquitos of 143, 333 (Norwegian), 235 and 248 squadrons was bounced by around 25 Fw 190s and Bf 109s as they made their way home. In the resulting combat, two Fw 190s were brought down and a third seen to be fleeing for home while on fire. One Mosquito from 235 Squadron was lost and a further three damaged but able to make it back to base. On 11 January, 14 Mosquitos and 18 Beaufighter escorts were again bounced by twelve Fw 190s and Bf 109s as they came in to attack merchant vessels at Flekkefjord — and once again everything disintegrated into a mass dogfight fought in thick cloud. The outcome was a Mosquito and a Beaufighter lost. In return, the Luftwaffe lost three fighters, with another claimed as a 'probable'.

It was the surprise operation of the 6lb nose gun from a Mosquito 'Tsetse' that eventually scared off German interceptors when another mass dogfight broke out on 15 January 1945. Sixteen Mosquitos from 143, 235 and 248 Squadrons had been tracking Lervik Harbour once again, sinking a combination of enemy merchant vessels and 'Flak Ships'. Having completed their raid, the Mosquitos found themselves under intense AA fire before being pounced on by nine Fw 190s. This time the enemy fighters took a vicious toll on the homeward-bound Mosquitos, shooting down six of them. It was to be the costliest raid ever undertaken from Banff. The CO of 143 Squadron was amongst the casualties, along with his navigator.

On April 9, 1945 the Banff Wing sank the U-804 and U-1065. Ten days later, a force of twenty-two Mosquitos using cannon and rockets sank the U-251 and damaged both the U-2502 and U-2335, as well as sinking an M-Class minesweeper.

"One U-boat blew up with a terrific flash and mushroom of smoke, throwing debris into the air which damaged four aircraft' — Banff Wing record book.

LEFT: Mosquito FB Mark XVIII, NT225 O, of No. 248 Squadron RAF Special Detachment based at Portreath, Cornwall, banking away from the camera while in flight, showing the 57mm Molins gun mounted underneath the nose

On 21 April, while out U-boat hunting in the Kattegat Sea, no less than 42 Mosquitos stumbled across a force of 16 Ju 88s. The Ju 88s, carrying torpedoes, had been sent to raid Allied shipping off Scotland. In the resulting aerial battle, which lasted less than five minutes, nine of the enemy bombers were destroyed and left behind, in the words of one Mosquito pilot *'a sea full of blazing aircraft'*.

Several more fled for their home base trailing smoke and flames. No Mosquitos were lost or even seriously damaged.

The Banff Strike Wing fought until the very last days of the war and flew some of the very last Mosquito missions. When the war ended, they had been operational for just nine months. Banff was closed as an operational station in 1946. The feature film *633 Squadron* — which features a hair-raising Mosquito Raid on Norway — was almost certainly inspired by the heroism of the Mosquito crews of the Banff Strike Wing.

'I shall never forget this day, as the force came out being attacked by the Germans, one plane chasing another, they were so low that they flew between two houses!'

Norwegian witness to the dogfight between Mosquitos of the Banff Strike Wing and German fighters, Boxing Day 1944

1945

'The Mosquito could get out of trouble faster than it got into it'

Wartime joke

CLOSING IN

By March 1945, Allied forces had successfully crossed the Rhine into Germany and were surging east. Despite it being obvious to all that the war was now lost, the Nazis fought on with increased fanaticism, in a nation now progressively being reduced to rubble and ruin. Bomber Command under Harris did not ease up either, striking again and again at what remained to the cities of the Reich. By May 1945 there were no less than eleven Mosquito squadrons serving with the Pathfinder force. Mosquitos continued to play all the roles they had established for themselves within Bomber Command, even as the Reich began to collapse. Tactics also changed to allow mass Mosquito attacks. On 21/22 March 1945, no less than 103 Mosquitos bombed Berlin. Later, 35 Mosquitos returned for 'Phase 2' of the raid.

BELOW: Bombing of the Gestapo headquarters in the Shellhus, Copenhagen, Denmark, in March 1945. A Mosquito pulling away from its bombing run is visible on the extreme left, centre

105 Squadron was still employed marking targets for the Heavies but did get the chance to launch their own daylight precision attacks. 139 Squadron, in its target marker role 'visited' Berlin on 33 consecutive nights during the winter and spring of 1944-1945. 163 Squadron also flew no less than 24 missions against Berlin in March 1945. In total, Mosquitos took part in raids on the German capital on 61 occasions during 1945. On 13 February 1945, 627 Mosquitos found they unopposed as they market targets in Dresden, and thereby became embroiled in the argument over the most contentious raids of the war.

OPERATION CARTHAGE – TRAGEDY IN COPENHAGEN

On 21 March 1945, in brilliant spring sunshine, eighteen Mosquito FB VIs from 21, 464 and 487 Squadrons set out from RAF Fersfield near Norwich to destroy Shell House in Copenhagen, which had been seized by the Nazis and used as Gestapo HQ in the Danish capital. With them came two further Mosquitos to film the raid and thirty RAF Mustang fighter escorts to hold off any marauding interceptors and to strafe and supress enemy anti-aircraft batteries. The attack had been launched after repeated requests for help from Danish resistance groups and agents from the SOE.

Once again Air Vice Marshal Basil Embry defied orders to take part in the raid, just has he had at Aarhus, adopting the flight suit of his dashing alter-ego *Wing Commander Smith*.

As the Mosquitos swept in just above the rooftops at 11.00am, Mosquito 'T-Tommy' flown by Wing Commander Peter Kleboe and Flying Officer Reginald Hall, struck a lamppost and veered off course crashing into a school — the Institut Jeanne d'Arc Roman Catholic girls school. Their bombs exploded and the school started burning just as the second and third waves made their bombing runs. Of these, a number of aircraft saw the fire and assumed that the school was the target, adding their bombs to the flames and killing more of the children below. 86 schoolchildren died in the blaze, as well as 18 members of staff, most of whom were nuns. A further 67 children were injured. Four Mosquitos and two of their Mustang escorts were lost during the raid, the losses due to anti-aircraft fire.

The only consolation was that other Mosquitos taking part in the raid had identified the correct target and destroyed the six storey Gestapo Headquarters, killing fifty-five Germans including members of the Gestapo as well as 47 Danish collaborators. Eighteen prisoners of the Gestapo escaped in the confusion.

Despite the tragic loss of the schoolchildren, the Danish resistance made a point of thanking the RAF for conducting the raid, as it had severely disrupted Gestapo operations and was believed to have saved the lives of many operatives targeted by the Nazis.

ABOVE: BBC journalist interviewing Squadron Leader E H Dunkley of 464 Squadron RAAF following a successful raid on Gestapo Headquarters, 'Shellhaus', Copenhagen, on 21 March 1945, by the Squadron's Mosquito aircraft

BELOW: Jeanne d'Arc School on fire

RIGHT: Mosquito FB.VI of 143 Squadron Royal Air Force being prepared for flight, Banff February 1945

THE TORTURE CASTLE

The last mission flown by Mosquitos against a Scandinavian target was flown on 1 April 1945 by six FB VIs of 140 Wing. Their destination was an agricultural college taken over by the Gestapo near Odense in Denmark. Officially called the the *Husmandsskolen,* the locals called it '*The Torture Castle'*.

The Mosquitos were joined on the raid by eight RAF Mustang fighters. The Mosquitos and their escorts now flew from Melsbroek in Belgium, thanks to the Allied advance since D-Day. Flying one of the Mosquitos, perhaps inevitably, was *'Wing Commander Smith',* the alter ego of Air Vice Marshall Basil Embry.

There was some difficulty in initially identifying the building due to the Germans erecting camouflaged netting, which led to locals becoming aware of aircraft circling overhead and consequently having time to find shelter. Bombing commenced at 4.30pm, with the Mosquitos dropping 500lb bombs from both their bomb bays and underwing

---

ABOVE: Air Vice-Marshal B E Embry, Air Officer Commanding No, 2 Group RAF, and his staff, study a scale model of a prospective target at Group Headquarters in Brussels. They are (left to right): Air Commodore D F W Atcherley, Senior Air Staff Officer; Group Captain P G Wykeham-Barnes, Group Captain Operations; Wing Commander H P Shallard, Group Intelligence Officer, and AVM Embry

racks, resulting In 2/3 of the *'Torture Castle'* being utterly demolished and the remaining parts gutted by fire.

Just one Mosquito was damaged in the raid when it was accidentally caught by its own bomb blast but managed to return to safety on a single engine.

'Wing Commander Smith' — or rather Air Vice Marshall Basil Embry, D.F.C., A.F.C. and four D.S.O.s, — went on to be knighted, promoted to Air Chief Marshall and to serve as Commander-in-Chief of Fighter Command between 1949 and 1953. In later life, he emigrated to Australia and passed away there in 1977.

'FIREBASH' – THE NAPALM RAIDS

Towards the end of the war, Mosquitos from 23 and 141 Squadrons were converted to carry napalm gel devices under their wings. 23 Squadron firebombed targets in Hohn and Flensburg on the night of 2-3 May 1945, while 169 Squadron used napalm against targets in Scleswig and Westerland that same night. 141 Squadron had already used Napalm dropped from 100 gallon drop-tanks on 18 April against an airfield situated near Munich. 13 of their Mosquitos later joined 23 Squadron on their Hohn and Flensburg raids.

BELOW: A de Havilland Mosquito PR Mk XVI of No. 140 Squadron RAF warms up its engines

BELOW: A demonstration by Mosquito fighters and Mustangs during an air display at a Royal Observer Corps official Stand Down ceremony at North Weald during the Second World War. 7th July 1945

THE DYING DAYS

Right up until when Adolf Hitler did the world a favour on 30 April 1945 and even beyond to 8 May when the Germans signed an unconditional surrender in Europe, Mosquitos were still flying their last missions in anger.

The veteran 21 Squadron flew their last mission on the night of 25-26 April, attacking road and rail targets in Wittenburg and Bad Oldsloe. That same night, 627 Squadron out of Woodhall Spa flew their last combat sorties, ranging against what were described as 'oil targets' in Tonsberg. 105 Squadron ceased fighting on the night on 2-3 May after bombing Eggebeck, but then flew further 'Manna' missions to mark airdrop locations for heavies parachuting in essential food supplies for starving civilians. 107 Squadron were out hunting until 26/27 April, shooting up any German troop concentrations they could find. 305 Squadron carried out similar combat sorties until 25-26 April. The following night, 613 Squadron flew their last combat missions, strafing German trains and rail junctions.

109 flew a split mission as late as 2-3 May, either bombing airfields at Eggebeck and Husum or else over Kiel marking targets for 128, 135, 142, 163 and 692 Squadron Mosquitos on bombing duties. B XVIs from 608 Squadron added to the carnage when 16 of their 'Fat-Belly' aircraft struck Kiel with 'Cookies' after which they retired from active war duties. Shipping in Kiel Harbour was still being attacked as late as 4 May by 404 Squadron RCAF and other units. Kiel was hit particularly heavily in the last days of the war to soften it up for advancing British troops and because German troop concentrations were preparing to evacuate north to Norway to continue the fight there.

BELOW: A U.S. Army Air Force de Havilland Canada Mosquito which was flown at the U.S. National Advisory Committee for Aeronautics (NACA) Langley Research Center, Virginia (USA), by test pilot Bill Gray during longitudinal stability and control studies of the aircraft in 1945. This aircraft was originally a Mosquito B Mk XX, the Canadian version of the Mosquito B Mk IV bomber aircraft. 145 were built, of which 40 were converted into photo-reconnaissance aircraft for the USAAF, which designated the planes F-8

ABOVE: A Banff Strike Wing Mosquito VI on final approach after another anti-shipping sortie, April 1945. Note the double-tiered rocket rails, which enabled the aircraft to carry drop tanks outboard of the engine nacelles

RIGHT: A de Havilland Mosquito of the RAF Banff Strike Wing attacking a convoy evacuating German troops in the Kattegat on 5 April 1945. A flak ship and a trawler were sunk

248 Squadron, took part in the sinking of U-boat U2359 on 2 May. Also hunting U-boats were the Tsetses' of 254 Squadron with their 6lb nose-mounted guns. During May 1945, they shared in operations which saw the destruction of no less than five U-boats. Shipping reconnaissance sorties were still being flown out of Eindhoven into Norwegian coastal waters by 140 Squadron until 7 May. On 9 May, six Mosquitos from 406 Squadron RCAF provided air over for the liberation of the Channel islands.

The Mosquito flew its very last combat mission of the Second World War in Europe on 21 May 1945, when a small number of aircraft from 143 and 248 Squadrons of the Banff Wing went hunting U-Boats off the coast of Scotland.

In the Far East, the Mosquito fighter-bombers of 110 Squadron were still in action on the 20 August, targeting hostile Japanese forces in Burma, despite Japan having officially surrendered on 14 August.

The Mosquitos of Bomber Command flew over 28,000 sorties during which they unleashed 35,000 tons of bombs. 193 Mosquitos of Bomber Command were lost in action — an overall loss rate of 0.7%.— the lowest losses of any aircraft flown by Bomber Command. Even against the most bitter opposition the Mosquito proved itself as a vital contributor to Bomber Command's war. It was even calculated that one Mosquito was worth as much as seven Lancasters. Bennett himself was a little dubious of the exact mathematics used to come to such a conclusion but reaffirmed that Mosquito's value was higher than *'any other aircraft ever produced in the history of flying'*.

778 de Havilland Mosquitos were shot down during the Second World War.

RIGHT: A de Havilland Mosquito FB Mark VI of 'A' Flight, No. 143 Squadron RAF, firing on two moored merchant vessels with rocket and cannon fire, during an attack by the Banff Strike Wing on concentrations of enemy shipping in Sandefjord, Norway. Two merchant vessels were sunk, and a tanker and three merchantmen damaged, for the loss of two Mosquitos out of 39 aircraft employed on the strike, 2 April 1945

'They think it's all over... it is now!'
Kenneth Wolstenholme, BBC sports commentator and ex-105 Mosquito Squadron pilot

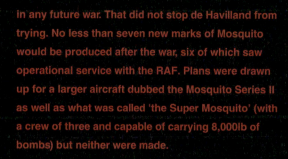

DECLINE AND FALL

By 1945 it was abundantly obvious that the Mosquito had seen its day. New jets like the British Gloster Meteor and the German Me 262 pointed the way to the future and there was little or no hope of improving the Mosquito further so that it might realistically compete in any future war. That did not stop de Havilland from trying. No less than seven new marks of Mosquito would be produced after the war, six of which saw operational service with the RAF. Plans were drawn up for a larger aircraft dubbed the Mosquito Series II as well as what was called 'the Super Mosquito' (with a crew of three and capable of carrying 8,000lb of bombs) but neither were made.

A total of 6,710 Mosquitos were built during the Second World War. Post-war production brought the final number to 7,781 all told. There were 51 versions. The very last Mosquito came off the production line on 15 November 1950 and was an NF 38 with the serial number VX916. It was almost ten years to the day since the first flight of the Mosquito prototype, which today is on display at the de Havilland Aircraft Museum next to the site of Salisbury Hall, along with two other surviving Mosquitos. Worldwide, only three Mosquitos are still airworthy and continue to fly. These are all in North America, but attempts are underway to restore a Mosquito to airworthy status in the UK. Some 30 grounded Mosquitos can be found in museums throughout the world.

SEA MOSQUITOS

811 Squadron were the first to be equipped with Sea Mosquitos. They were based at Ford in Sussex. The first of fifteen FB VI variants arrived in September 1945 and the following year these were joined by TR 33s. By 1947, the squadron had been disbanded. Sea Mosquitos then mainly served with Fleet Requirement Units, being handed out to different squadrons for specific duties.

LEFT: Close-up of front of de Havilland DH.98 Mosquito FB VI at Omaka Aviation Heritage Centre's "Dangerous Skies" exhibition, with the cockpit access door open and the four .303 machine guns in the nose visible

The Mosquito TR 37, differing really only by new improved radar in its nose succeeded the TR 33. Only fourteen were ever produced by the new de Havilland factory at Chester and served with 703 Squadron.

A STATE OF CONFUSION

Post-war, the new Labour government were more than eager to claim their 'peace dividend'. Building new housing and funding the newly conceived 'Welfare State' would cost money. As might have been expected, the move to dismantle the wartime RAF began with a degree of haste and no little amount of confusion. Many squadrons were disbanded and their aircraft simply sent to the scrapyards.

The Mosquito benefitted from this. Having been forced into parsimony, the RAF tried to make do with whatever they had to hand. In moves which eerily echoed events at the end of the Great War, Mosquitos were sent out to far flung areas of the Empire to help keep order. There were now Mosquitos to be found in Egypt, Palestine, India, Iraq, Kenya, Aden, Hong Kong, the Sudan, Singapore and Malaya, amongst other far distant outposts.

There was also, inevitably, some confusion amongst all the juggling and squadron renumbering. 609 Squadron for example — who had spent the war flying Spitfires and Typhoons — suddenly found themselves being converted to fly Mosquito NF XXX's in May 1946, only to be switched back to Spitfires again in April 1948. 45 Squadron posted to the Far East had their Mosquito FB VIs snatched away in favour of Beaufighter X's in November 1945 — only to have some Mosquitos returned to them in 1948. 98 Squadron only received Mosquitos after hostilities had ceased, while 605 Squadron (AAF) were down on the books as a night fighter squadron, but were mostly equipped with Mosquito trainers. 22 Squadron were supplied with Mosquitos to replace their Beaufighters out in Singapore on 1 May 1946 only to be disbanded in August that year, flying them for just over three months in total. '504 Squadron were designated

ABOVE: Mosquito FB.VI TA122 UP-G - Built at Hatfield in 1945 and entered service in March that year, initially serving with 605 Squadron in Belgium and Holland and later with 4 Squadron in Germany. Withdrawn from service in 1950, the fuselage became an instructional airframe at Delft Univesity in Holland from 1951 to 1970. After seven years in the Royal Netherlands Air Force museum, it came to Salisbury Hall. The airframe was restored using the mainplane from Sea Mosquito TR.33 'TW233' which was recovered from Israel in 1980. Almost complete, she has been painted in original 605 Squadron markings

as a bomber squadron but were supplied with night fighters instead. Boston squadron No 55 were finally given Mosquito XXVIs in July 1946 but were disbanded before they could even become operational. Everywhere it seemed that squadrons were being renumbered, disbanded, and reformed only to become disbanded again. '*Make Do and Mend*' had quickly descended into '*Muddle Through*'.

As the Mosquitos were phased out, they were replaced by jets - Vampires, Meteors and Canberras.

FIREDOG

After the war with Japan ceased, around 350 RAF Mosquitos remained in south-east Asia as new conflicts and tensions sprung up. Mosquito fighter-bombers from 47, 84 and 110 RAF Squadrons assisted the Dutch in fighting pro-independence forces in Indonesia. Although mainly assigned to reconnaissance and escort duties they also launched a number of ground attack combat missions and continued offering support until March 1946.

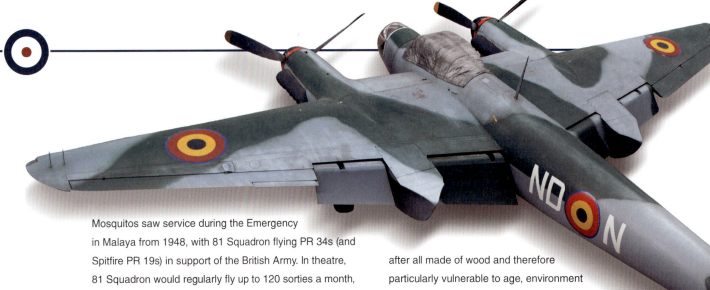

Mosquitos saw service during the Emergency in Malaya from 1948, with 81 Squadron flying PR 34s (and Spitfire PR 19s) in support of the British Army. In theatre, 81 Squadron would regularly fly up to 120 sorties a month, totalling some 6,619 sorties during the course of the Emergency and only flying their last operational combat sortie there on 15 December 1955, when a Mosquito PR. 34A (RG3 14) flown by Flying Officer 'Collie' Knox and his navigator Flying Officer Tommy Thompson conducted a photo-reconnaissance mission over the jungle searching for communist encampments. Meteor PR 10s replaced them in the theatre.

THE RAF - LAST DAYS

The final version of the Mosquito bomber, the B 35, made its first test flight at the end of March 1945, but the war was over by the time it came off the production line. It nevertheless served with the RAF as a bomber until 1954. The last fighters ended their RAF service in 1950, while PR versions were superseded by the jet engined Canberra in 1951. Mosquito T III trainers continued in service until 1953. After this, a number of B 35s served as humble target towers until May 1963. The last ever operational RAF Mosquitos were TT 35's and T 3III' s belonging to No. 3 Civilian Anti-Aircraft Co-Operation Unit (CAACU). These too served as target tugs until the very last one was finally retired in May 1963.

THE FAILING AND THE FAR-FLUNG

Way back in 1938, when the Mosquito was just a glint in Geoffrey de Havilland's eye, it was fully understood that the Mosquito would have a potentially short life. It was after all made of wood and therefore particularly vulnerable to age, environment and insect. At the time, no-one cared. How long would a war take? And how long could a warplane expect to survive in the maelstrom anyway?

Post war, the Mosquito began to age poorly and misbehaved mightily. Despite this, there was still considerable demand for the Mosquito from foreign air forces who were desperate to have something — anything — to fly in the new post-war world. And so the Mosquitos went on sale, whether through government bodies or entrepreneurial private intermediaries who sometimes had just the whiff of the spiv about them.

Sweden purchased 60 night fighters (designated J30s) and flew them until 1954. In that time, a full third crashed or broke down due to mechanical issues. Norway's 333 Squadron brought 18 fighter-bombers back after their wartime service with Coastal Command which were later converted to night fighters. After a fatal accident

ABOVE: De Havilland DH.98 Mosquito NF.30 'MB24 - ND-N' - This is one of only two remaining night-fighter Mosquitos, the other being NF.II 'HJ711' at Elvington in Yorkshire, UK. This late model example was built as RK952 for the RAF, but transferred to the Belgian Air Force in 1953 as 'MB24'. Retired in 1957, it was preserved as part of what is known as the Brussels Air Museum, although it is actually the Air and Space Section of the Royal Museum of the Armed Forces and Military History, Brussels, Belgium

grounded the entire Norwegian Mosquito force in 1951, the Norwegians took the decision to take them out of service the following year.

Turkey imported 96 fighter-bombers, mainly for use in an anti-shipping capacity. Several structural failures and crashes attributed to problems with the old wood glue led the Turks to minimise the use of their Mosquitos and they were finally withdrawn altogether in 1953, when they were perhaps predictably replaced by American F-84G Thunderjets.

South Africa chose the Mosquito for its photo-reconnaissance abilities, buying 14 PR XVI/XIs, but the Mosquito suffered because of the African climate and were withdrawn sooner than planned after a number of structural failures.

The Belgium post-war economy was so bad that not much use was made of their Mosquitos and restrictions were placed on how many hours they could fly due to costs. An exception was made for participating in NATO events. The aircraft received were also received in generally poor condition and six aircraft were lost from their original force of twenty-two NF 30s due to accidents. The Belgian Air Force finally withdrew the Mosquito from service in 1956 to be replaced by Gloster Meteors.

THE MOSQUITO STRUGGLES ON

Some air forces had more luck with their Mosquitos than others. Yugoslavia reinforced its air force with eighty fighter-bombers, sixty night fighters and three trainers which flew in some capacity or other until 1963.

After seeing an awful lot of the Mosquito in action while under occupation, France re-equipped its post war air force with 57 fighter bombers, 29 reconnaissance versions, 23 night fighters and a small number of bombers. Only two fell apart in mid-air while being delivered. Some saw service against insurrectionists in French IndoChina (Vietnam) between 1947 and 1949 as part of Corse Squadron. Even Burma bought a flight of FB VIs, in 1955 for use against rebel groups. Other customers included Czechoslovakia and the Dominican Republic. In the case of Czechoslovakia, some of the Mosquitos needed to be refitted with German machine guns and cannon because of a lack of available British ammunition. The Mosquito's service with the Czechs came to an abrupt end when the Russians, who occupied the country, asked where the aircraft had come from. After being told it was Britain, their masters immediately gave orders for all the Mosquitos

BELOW: Mosquito CF-HMS purchased by Lynn Garrison arrives in Calgary, February, 1964

ABOVE: W4050 being restored at the de Havilland Aircraft Heritage Centre near St Albans

in the country to be burned — which they duly were. The Canadian Air Force carried on commissioning aircraft from its own factory after the war as did the RAAF, which also took 75 fighter-bombers and photo-reconnaissance aircraft from Britain.

Australia used its wartime production of Mosquitos to use PR versions for a complete aerial survey of the continent. Two thirds of Australia had been extensively surveyed and mapped by the time the flight was disbanded in 1953. New Zealand meanwhile received eighty Mosquitos which comprised two bomber-reconnaissance squadrons until they were finally replaced by de Havilland Vampire jets.

America purchased twenty six B XX's from Canada to serve with USAAF. These were converted for photo-reconnaissance duties and were flown by 375 Servicing Squadron over in England. The original Canadian aircraft were eventually replaced by PR XVIs.

LIN TAI YU

Starting in 1947, Canada exported virtually all of its surplus stock - around 200 Mosquitos - at bargain prices to serve with the Nationalist Chinese air force in its fight with communist insurgents. Many were damaged in transit and perhaps as many as sixty others were lost due to pilot error in training. Chinese pilots were said to be frightened by the Mosquito, as it was significantly bigger than anything they were used to — some to the extent that they had to be let go during training. To try and stop this, a Mosquito FB was converted into a trainer only capable of taxiing — but the Chinese managed to wreck this too, taxiing it straight into a large hole. A further, small number of surviving Mosquitos were lost when their crews simply defected to the Communist Chinese. There aircraft were subsequently then used against Nationalist forces. When the Communists finally overran the country, surviving Mosquitos were rescued by being flown off to Taiwan.

Nevertheless, the pilots actually capable of flying it loved the Mosquito calling it the *'Lin Tai Yu'* after a legendary Chinese Empress who was both beautiful and wicked.

THE GUST RESEARCH UNIT

The post-war world was starting to anticipate pressurised high flying civilian airliners and to ensure safety by better understanding turbulence. The Ministry of Supply set up the GRU (Gust Research Unit) at Cranfield to conduct meteorological research. Two Mosquito PR 34s were assigned to the unit in June 1947 and spent the next two years operated by BEA bringing back data from the turbulence 'hot spots' they discovered for scientists to better understand the phenomena. Missions were typically flown at heights between 15,000 and 37,000 feet.

MOSQUITOS VERSUS THE RAF

As early as 1947, the Royal Egyptian Air Force seized the opportunity to buy ex-RAF Mosquitos (as well as Spitfires and Lancasters) to add some relatively modern muscle to its essentially obsolete fleet. The Mosquitos comprised 22 fighter bombers (designated FB. 51s) and 16 night fighters (NF 52s), all supplied with radar. Attempts were made to make them more suitable for use in the Egyptian climate and included Bristol Hercules 100 radial engines.

Just over a year later, these aircraft were being used in hostilities against the RAF. On 14 May 1948, as the State of Israel came into being, a coalition of Arab nations attacked and tried to invade. Egyptian Mosquitos blitzed the RAF airfield at Ramat David and destroyed several RAF aircraft on the ground. Eventually having identified the Mosquitos markings as Egyptian, the RAF responded in force and destroyed almost every last warplane the REAF possessed. Due to the quirks of international politics, Britain and Egypt would soon be friends again and by 1949 Britain was actually replenishing the REAF with Gloster Meteor jets and de Havilland Vampires. (They fell out again in 1952, and Egypt switched to Soviet jets instead).

MORE MOSQUITOS OVER THE HOLY LAND

The actual number of Mosquitos purchased by the fledgling nation of Israel is still shrouded in secrecy but it is widely thought to have eventually been as many as 300. During the Arab-Israeli War of 1948-49, they had just two precious Mosquitos which were used for photo-reconnaissance duties. (a third one crashed on its way to Israel due to its poor condition).

At least 65 more were obtained in 1951. These were ex-French Air Force Mosquitos passed over to the Israeli Air Force for $13,000 each (if they were in good condition) and as little as $200 each for ones only good for spare parts. Many Mosquitos obtained by the IAF were in less than trustworthy condition, and it was said that ground crews had to play the flute next to each aircraft every morning to lure the worms out from the aircraft's wooden frame. More were purchased from the Royal Navy.

BELOW: De Havilland Mosquito TR33, Israel Air Force

RIGHT: Built in April 1945 but immediately went in to store until May 1952 when she went to Brooklands Aviation at Sywell for conversion to a TT.35 target tug. After two years operational towing, she went back in to store in December 1954. In September 1959 she was delivered to No.3 Civilian Anti-Aircraft Co-operation Unit (CAACU) based at Exeter where she remained on strength until May 1963. She then moved to the Central Flying School at Little Rissington for use as a display aircraft. The target towing equipment was removed and she was repainted in camouflage. During 1963 she took part in filming '633 Squadron' wearing the serial 'HJ682' and coded 'HT-B'. She continued to make occasional display flights until October 1965, when she was grounded and stored. She came to Cosford in 1969 and has remained here since. In 1988 she was painted to represent Mosquito XX 'AZ-E' of 627 sqn, in which Wing Commander Guy Gibson was killed on 20th September 1944. She is on display in the 'War in the Air' hangar. RAF Museum, Cosford, Shropshire, UK

The Israeli Mosquitos again mainly served as photo-reconnaissance aircraft flying missions to gather intelligence on hostile Arab nations. Despite many attempts to bring down Israeli Mosquito spy planes using MiG 15s and other supposedly superior jet fighters, not one succeeded. Mosquitos flew their last ever combat missions with the Israeli Air Force during Operation Kadesh - the Suez Crisis of 1956 - when thirteen Mosquitos were taken out of storage for use. IAF Mosquitos flew in a reconnaissance role once more to photograph Egyptian air fields and the anticipated British and French invasion beaches. When the conflict

turned 'hot', Mosquitos serving as part of the IAF 110th Squadron were used mainly as ground attack aircraft to strike at enemy troop concentrations and vehicle columns in the Sinai Desert, but also served to fly escort for the IAF's two Flying Fortresses. Plans were made for Mosquitos to attack and sink the Egyptian destroyer Ibrahim Al Awal but the strike was cancelled. Two aircraft were lost in the fighting.

The Mosquito ended its service in the IAF in 1957, when the aircraft were de-activated and then installed in children's playgrounds in Kibbutzim all over Israel.

SPARTANS

Ten Canadian Mosquitos were purchased for high altitude (up to 35,000 feet) aerial survey work by Spartan Air Services of Ottawa in 1954, modified to carry an extra fuel tank, a third crew member (the photographer) and to have three camera windows inside the fuselage. More P.35s were later purchased by Spartan from Britain. These were used not only to conduct photographic surveys of Canada and the Arctic but also found work as far afield as Central and South America and Africa.

Two B.25s were purchased to use in Air Racing and a number of other Mosquitos were bought for prospective world record speed or distance flights. Relatively few were ever flown, due to fast developing mechanical and structural issues.

CIA

Mosquitos registered as civil aircraft were sometimes used by the CIA for operations in South East Asia during the Vietnam War. The CIA were also known to have operated at least one Mosquito on clandestine information gathering missions over South America.

633 SQUADRON

In 1963, ten Mosquito TT 35s and T IIIs were purchased for private use in the film *633 Squadron*, which followed a vital mission by RAF Mosquitos to destroy a German 'Heavy Water' production facility in a Norwegian Fjord. The aircraft were based at Bovingdon, with the majority of the aerial filming being conducted in relatively quiet skies of Norfolk. (The '*Enemy Coast Ahead*' is actually The Wash). Scottish locations, including Loch Ness, were chose to depict Norway.

RIGHT: American actor Cliff Robertson (1923 - 2011) as 'Wing Commander Roy Grant' on the set of British war film '633 Squadron', UK, 31st July 1963

ABOVE: Owned by Tony Agar and based at the Yorkshire Air Museum since the mid 1980's, this is a restoration of a de Havilland Mosquito NF.11. The restoration is also unique as it's the only existing version of this variant in the world. Parts have been obtained from Canada, America, New Zealand and Australia